OLD SOUTHWEST/NEW SOUTHWEST

Watercolor by N. Scott Momaday, painted to accompany his essay "Landscape with Words in the Foreground."

Essays on a Region and Its Literature

OLD SOUTHWEST
NEW SOUTHWEST

Edited by Judy Nolte Lensink

Tucson: The Tucson Public Library, 1987

CREDITS: The Photographs on pages ix, 3, 6, 16, 27, 48, 62, 93, 100, 112, 121, 145 and 162 are by Cynthia Farah (copyrighted in her name); on page 38 by Lance Fairchild; on page 133 by Judy Nolte Lensink. The cover art is by David Maier.

Library of Congress Cataloging-in-Publication Data

Old Southwest/new Southwest.

Papers from the Old Southwest/New Southwest Conference held Nov. 14-17, 1985 in Tucson, Ariz. and sponsored by the Tucson Public Library and the National Endowment for the Humanities.
Bibliography: p.
1. American literature—Southwestern States—History and criticism—Congresses. 2. Southwestern States in literature—Congresses. 3. Southwestern States—Intellectual life—Congresses. 4. Southwest, Old—Congresses. 5. Southwest, New—Congresses. I. Lensink, Judy Nolte, 1948- II. Old Southwest/New Southwest Conference (1985: Tucson, Ariz.) III. Tucson Public Library. IV. National Endowment for the Humanities.
PS277.04 1987.   810'.9'979   86-27260

Distributed by the University of Arizona Press, 1615 East Speedway, Tucson, Arizona 85719.
Production of this book has been made possible by a grant from the National Endowment for the Humanities. Printed in the United States of America.

ISBN 0-9617849-0-3

CONTENTS

JUDY NOLTE LENSINK

INTRODUCTION

Between the Rio Colorado and the upper course of the Rio Grande lies
the Land of Journeys' Ending . . . . Go far enough on any of its trails,
and you begin to see how the world was made.
—Mary Austin

The goal of the Writers of the Purple Sage Project, supported by
the National Endowment for the Humanities since 1983, is to
understand how the Myth of the West was made. The project was
conceived by Kathleen Dannreuther and Jere Stephan of the Tucson
Public Library and by Karen Dahood of the Arizona Historical Society.
The Writers of the Purple Sage programs and publications have
engaged many readers in an exploration of the literary roots of the
Southwestern mystique.[1]
   Project scholars studied early popular literature about the
Southwest written between 1875 and 1925 in their search for the origins
of a national myth. Their work covered four areas: Out West (adventure
literature); The Golden West (promotional writing); Indian Country
(literature about Native Americans); Down Mexico Way (depictions of
life in Mexico).
   During their project research, the Library staff and the scholars
realized that the literature that created the Southwestern mystique did
not end in the modern era. In fact, through other media such as film
the image of the Old Southwest—full of spacious landscapes,
stereotypical characters and endless action—was still powerful and had

attracted many of us to this region for our own journeys' ending. Project Director Teresa Turner and Tucson Public Library Coordinator of Educational Services Kathleen Dannreuther requested additional funds from the NEH to expand our study to contemporary Southwestern literature. We wished to reach the wider national audience that had shown an interest in Writers of the Purple Sage materials and to involve more scholars and writers in the project.

And this is how a conference—OLD SOUTHWEST/NEW SOUTHWEST— was made. We wanted to follow the trail of Southwestern literature into the present to see how past literary images affect current writers and readers.

There are many questions and issues that both trouble and stimulate those who study Southwestern literature and these provided a foreground for OLD SOUTHWEST/NEW SOUTHWEST:

What, indeed is this region we call the Southwest? Is it a mappable geographic zone, a unique amalgam of cultures, a sense of place, a state of mind?

How can one hope to define as a single region a land that contains within it both Indian hogans and urban highrises?

Who speaks for the Southwest, a triptych of rich Anglo, Hispanic and Indian cultures?

What determines the writer's roots and the authenticity of voice— nativity in the Southwest; a conscious choice of this region as one's adopted homeland; artistic empathy?

Is the Southwest's position on the borderland of the publishing and literary world a zone of disregard—or the last open space in which to roam the farthest regions of the imagination?

What do Southwestern writers have to say to and about America? Is our literature interesting only to ourselves, or are our themes universal?

The OLD SOUTHWEST/NEW SOUTHWEST conference was held November 14-17, 1985, at the Westward Look Resort in Tucson. Arizona. The conference presentations, from which the essays in this book were selected, began with an exploration of our literary roots. From there we moved to an examination and critique of our region's literary history and its image in film and popular literature. We ended with discussions of issues facing contemporary Southwestern writers: what is their role in our survival as a region and how do they themselves survive in the publishing world?

The essays in OLD SOUTHWEST/NEW SOUTHWEST follow the same trail of reflection, critical analysis, and foresight. N. Scott Momaday

Judy Lensink, Project Director of Writers of the Purple Sage, and author Frank Waters at the honors ceremony that closed the OLD SOUTHWEST/NEW SOUTHWEST conference.

begins with "Landscape with Words in the Foreground," his thoughts on the very origins of American literature and the organic relationship between the writer and the Southwestern land.

Frank Waters, who has been writing about this region for over sixty years, talks in "Roots and Literary Influences" about the challenge of getting books rooted in the authentic Southwestern experience published and accepted.

Rolando Hinojosa-Smith then argues persuasively that our concept of American literature should be opened up to "The Other American Literatures" by Hispanic writers who can enrich our vision.

Arrell Morgan Gibson's essay, "The Author as Image Maker for the Southwest," provides an essential literary history of the depiction of this region by writers.

Southwestern literary history is then critiqued and enlarged in "Angles of Vision: Enhancing Our Perspectives on the Southwest" by Janice Monk and Vera Norwood, who analyze women's literature.

Tey Diana Rebolledo continues this expansion in "Hispanic Women Writers of the Southwest: Tradition and Innovation," her exploration of two generations of writers.

David Lavender tackles historical novels about the Southwest by Willa Cather and Wallace Stegner in his critique, "The Tyranny of Facts," which questions the balance between good history and a good story.

In "Hollywood and the West: Mexican Images in American Films, 1894-1983," Juan R. García surveys the connection between historical events, myth, and stereotypes of Hispanic peoples in Westerns.

"The Failure of Western Writing" presents William Eastlake's contribution to the debate over the universality of regional literature and the value of the Western experience to writers.

John Nichols calls for literature of commitment in "The Writer as Revolutionary," using examples and observations from his involvement with issues in New Mexico.

Rudolfo Anaya reflects on his training in traditional American literature and its effect on his art in "An American Chicano in King Arthur's Court."

Thomas J. Lyon proposes in "Beyond the Frontier Mind" that the best Southwestern literature presents a new and instructive way of looking at the American land.

Charles Bowden, who writes about both the urban and the unpopulated Southwest, questions the power of environmental literature in "Useless Deserts and Other Goals."

In "Writers of the Purple Figwort," Ann Zwinger closely defines the differences in wilderness writing and talks about her experiences leading to a career of exploring the Southwest.

Reyner Banham argues that neither environmental writers nor the other users of the desert are realistic in "Having It All: Partisan Greed and Possession of the Desert."

Finally, the premier historian of Southwestern letters, Lawrence Clark Powell, closes with his personal reflections, "The Fountain and the Well: Sources of Southwestern Literature."

While no publication can recreate the excitement of the interaction between writers, scholars and listeners that occurred at the OLD SOUTH-WEST/NEW SOUTHWEST conference, we hope these essays will provoke fresh thinking about our region and its literature. For this is how a strong and authentic Southwestern voice is made.

ACKNOWLEDGMENTS

I have enjoyed directing the Writers of the Purple Sage project and the OLD SOUTHWEST/NEW SOUTHWEST conference, for I have learned much about my adopted home, the Southwest, through its books.

I have met scholars and writers from across the nation who are concerned and informed about the state of Southwestern literature. Although our conversations often centered on conference and essay details, I also enjoyed our many talks about writing, wonderful Southwestern places, and new works in progress.

Much of the praise for the success of OLD SOUTHWEST/NEW SOUTH-WEST conference goes to the large group of people who helped plan the conference and supported it with hard work. Those who guided the conception of the conference were Kathleen Dannreuther (Tucson Public Library); Bruce Dinges (*Arizona and the West*); Teresa L. Turner (my predecessor as Director); and Larry Evers (English Department, University of Arizona).

Throughout the Writers of the Purple Sage project we have been advised and encouraged by Dr. Thomas Phelps, our Program Officer at the National Endowment for the Humanities. His interest in Southwestern literature and his sound suggestions made the OLD SOUTHWEST/NEW SOUTHWEST Conference possible.

Tucson Public Library support came from Director Marcia King; Deputy Director Susan Goldberg; Administrator for Library Services Jere Stephan; Public Information Officer Kelly Balisle-Goodrich;

Coordinator of Educational Services Kathleen Dannreuther. Special thanks for the success of the conference goes to Rosemary Welsch, Secretary of the Writers of the Purple Sage Project.

Those who worked tirelessly during the conference include Roxane Martell-Jones and volunteers Kelly Balisle-Goodrich, Kathleen Dannreuther, Susan Goldberg, Kris Hillier, Betty Lenz, Jo McGinnis, Mary Robinson, Karen Phelps, Viola Spelbring, Agnes Stahlschmidt, Jere Stephan, G. Chris Stern, Teresa Turner and Kathy Young.

This book was designed and produced by A. Tracy Row. The cover art for this book is by David Maier, who won a competition for OLD SOUTHWEST/NEW SOUTHWEST poster design held at the University of Arizona with the cooperation of Professor Carl Heldt. Most of the photographs are by Cynthia Farah of El Paso, who has captured many of the Southwest's literary greats with her camera. Rosemary Welsch tirelessly typed the manuscripts for this book; her research and suggestions have improved it. Jean Schwartz carefully perused every essay in OLD SOUTHWEST/NEW SOUTHWEST to perfect our publication and I thank her.

ENDNOTES

[1]Because the Library and Endowment are committed to accessible public programming, portfolios containing primary literature about the Southwest, bibliographies, scholarly essays and programming ideas were disseminated throughout our region as part of the Purple Sage project. In addition, several Southwestern writers and scholars gave presentations about their work, and field trips were organized to such places as northern Arizona for the Hopi Snake Dance and Cananea, Sonora, Mexico, to trace the origins of the Mexican Revolution. An award-winning series of programs on Southwestern literature was broadcast on many National Public Radio stations.

OLD SOUTHWEST/NEW SOUTHWEST

N. SCOTT MOMADAY

LANDSCAPE WITH WORDS IN THE FOREGROUND

By means of the title above I wish to indicate a certain equation that has become more and more important to me. I wish to suggest painting as well as writing as a clear reflection of the deepest reality of the Southwest, for I am a painter as well as a writer. These two expressions of my spirit, painting and writing, are not unrelated, I believe. As a matter of fact, I have come to believe that they are so closely related as to be indivisible.

One of the definitions—perhaps the most basic of all—of the word "write" is this: "to draw or form by scoring or incising a surface." Imagine somewhere in the prehistoric distance a man. He holds up in his hand a crude instrument, a brand, perhaps, or something like a daub or a broom, bearing pigment, and he fixes the wonderful image in his mind's eye to a wall of rock. In that instant he accomplishes really and symbolically the beginning of art. That man, apart from his remarkable creation, is all but impossible to recall from the remote past, and yet he is there in our human parentage, in our racial memory. In our modern, sophisticated terms, he is primitive and illiterate, and in the whole reach of time he is utterly without distinction—except, he draws. And his contribution to posterity is immeasurable. He makes a profound difference in our lives, on us who succeed him by thousands of years. For all the stories of all the world proceed from the moment he makes his mark. All literatures issue from his hand.

Language and literature involve sacred matter and sacred places, places of deepest mystery and ancient vision. Among sacred places in

1

America, there is one that comes to my mind as I think of that anonymous man who painted upon the face of rock. At Barrier Canyon, Utah, there are some twenty sites upon which are preserved prehistoric rock art. One of these, known as the Great Gallery, is particularly arresting. Among arched alcoves and long ledges of rock is a wide sandstone wall on which are drawn large, tapering anthropomorphic forms colored in dark red pigment. There on the ancient picture plane is a procession of gods approaching inexorably from the earth. They are informed with irresistible power; they are beyond our understanding, masks, if you will, of infinite possibility. We do not know what they mean, but we know that we are involved in their meaning. They persist through time in the imagination, and we cannot doubt that they are invested with the very essence of language, the language of story and myth. They are two thousand years old, more or less, and they remark as closely as anything can the origin of American literature.

Let me point in my writings to two brief passages in which this equation of words in the landscape is applied to my memory of growing up in the American Southwest. The first passage is from *The Names*, an autobiographical narrative that was published in our bicentennial year by Harper & Row.

Monument Valley: red to blue; great violet shadows, planes and prisms of light. Once, from a window in the wall of a canyon, I saw men on horseback, far below, two of them, moving slowly into gloaming, and they were singing. They were so far away that I could only barely see them, and their small, clear voices lay very lightly and for a long time on the distance between us.

The valley is vast. When you look out over it, it does not occur to you that there is an end to it. You see the monoliths that stand away in space, and you imagine that you have come upon eternity. They do not appear to exist in time. You think: I see that time comes to an end on this side of the rock, and on the other side there is nothing forever. I believe that only in DINÉ BIZAAD, the Navajo language, which is endless, can this place be described, or even indicated in its true character. Just there is the center of an intricate geology, a whole and unique landscape which includes Utah, Colorado, Arizona, and New Mexico. The most brilliant colors in the earth are there, I believe, and the most beautiful and extraordinary land forms—and surely the coldest, clearest air, which is run through with pure light.

The long wall of red rocks which extends eastward and for miles from Gallup, New Mexico, describes something of the hard, bright beauty of the continent at its summit. The Continental Divide runs down and

N. Scott Momaday is a Pulitzer Prize-winning novelist and an artist who has exhibited his work internationally. He teaches in the English Department at the University of Arizona.

intersects this wall at Coolidge. In the long reach of country which lies between Coolidge and the red rock wall there are cattle and sheep, rabbits and roadrunners, all delightful to a child. They were small and nearly silent in the distance, and they bore upon the land in an easy, nearly discreet way. They seemed not to intrude, that is, as machines do in so many of the landscapes of our time; or perhaps this is merely MY sense of things, having long ago taken that countryside as I found it, cut through with glinting rails and puffing trains. Like the red wall above them, they made an ordinary stratum on the scene. I try to imagine that large expanse without them, but then there is a flaw in the design. For in my mind's eye, too, a train stitches black across the plain.

The second passage is from a work in progress, a novel which is tentatively entitled *Set*. Set is the name of the main character, a name which means "bear" in the Kiowa language. The story is, at its center, about a boy who turns into a bear, and it is based upon an ancient myth in the oral tradition. In this passage, Set has returned to a sacred, ancestral home. The narration is his own.

Later I wanted to stretch my legs, and I went for a walk. It was just past six o'clock, and the heat had fallen off. There was a breeze, very light, and warm rather than cool, but it felt good and it smelled of leaves and grass.... The sun was low, and the light had softened; there was a copper tint upon everything, even the shadows. The bare earth seemed saturated with the soft, sanguine light. I could not remember ever having seen earth of that color; it was red, earlier a flat, brick red, now deeper, like that particular Conti crayon that is red and brown, like old blood, at the same time; or Catlinite, the color of my father's name. I walked to the creek, along Cradle Creek for a mile or so. The growth there was dense, and the water was red like the earth, and the current was very slow, almost imperceptible. The bitch had followed me. I spoke to her now and then, but she paid me no mind; she ambled along in her own ancient and maternal perception of the universe, I supposed. I had the sense that she did not accompany me; she merely happened to be travelling the same path.

I had a strange feeling there, as if some ancestral intelligence had been awakened in me for the first time. There in the wild growth and the glowing earth, in the muddy water at my feet, was something profoundly original and originative. I could not put my finger on it, but it was there. It was itself genesis, I thought, not genesis in the public domain, not the Old Testament, by MY genesis. I wanted to see my father there in the shadows of Cradle Creek, the child he once was, myself in him. But I couldn't; there was only something like a photograph, old and indefinite, in my mind's eye.

Then somewhere something moved. The motion was sudden and without sound. I had caught only a glimpse of it out of the corner of my eye. And then I was looking hard across the creek, into a small brake. Dusk had entered there; the dim light was like smoke; the foliage hung still and black. A time passed in which I held my breath, listening, searching. "Well, whatever it was, it's gone now," I said to the bitch. She had set her head and was peering intently into the same recess. The hair on her nape was raised.

When I look back over these passages, the two of them some ten years apart in time, I am struck by a common quality which informs them, a point of view, it may be, or an irresistible sense of place. It happens that the character Set is an artist, a painter, as I am a painter. He sees the world in a particular way, in terms of lines, and shapes, and shadows, and forms—in terms of foregrounds and backgrounds and middle distances, in terms of color and light. In both passages there is a strong accent upon the concept of the mind's eye, an emphasis of which I was not aware until I had put the passages together.

No doubt you have already taken the point I am trying to make: that the elements of place and vision, as they are realized in the imagination, in the mind's eye, if you will, form the aesthetic equation that is art. And I am speaking of particulars, not of any place, nor of any vision, but of sacred ground and of ancient vision.

As an artist, I want to say: in the landscape of my homeland let me place an offering of words in the foreground. And in this act, which is holy, let me stand in the place of that man who touched the wonderful image in his mind's eye to the wall of rock. It is appropriate; it is good.

Indian literature contains & conveys images of sacred ground & ancient vision — land & myth

Frank Waters has written twenty-one books and has been awarded honorary doctorates by seven universities in the West. He was nominated for the Nobel Prize for Literature.

FRANK WATERS

ROOTS AND
LITERARY INFLUENCES

I think that I, like all writers whether they admit it or not, have been consciously or unconsciously influenced by everything I've read. But a writer's roots must go deeper than into the wealth of past literature produced by a multitude of talented writers. He must attune his antennae to new views on old ideas, to new people and situations, to the land itself. These sometimes present conflicts with presently accepted views and give him trouble. Such has been my own experience. I shall try to illustrate it here with a few examples from my own writing over the past fifty years.

My roots go deep into this land. I was born in Colorado Springs, at the foot of Pikes Peak. Some of my earliest childhood memories are of the Ute Indians who were permitted each summer to return from their reservation to their old homeland here, pitching their smoke-gray conical lodges on the mesa west of town. The encampment was shunned by the respectable citizens of town. But my father was a close friend of the Ute elders, and often drove me in his buckboard to sit with them around the evening campfire. I didn't understand their language, but their strong faces and dignified bearing in the flamelight spoke more clearly.

Their mode of thinking, their way of looking at everything as I came to know it, seemed more natural to me than that taught in my Anglo schools and churches. Throughout the Southwest, Mexico and Guatemala, I have always somehow been associated with Indian people. So it isn't strange that many of my twenty-one published books have been about Indian life, culture, and religious ceremonialism.

7

The Man Who Killed the Deer, first published in 1942, was based on Pueblo Indian life, particularly that of Taos Pueblo. The novel was an immediate flop and quickly went out of print. No one was interested in Indians; the traditional Anglo prejudice against them was still prevalent. But the novel became a collector's item, and more small printings were issued, with later translations in French, German, Dutch, and Swedish. Not for years did it gain a measure of popularity.

A decade later my nonfiction *Masked Gods: Navajo and Pueblo Ceremonialism* (1950) created trouble for me. It was commissioned by the University of New Mexico Press, which rejected the manuscript when it was submitted because the book didn't adhere to orthodox anthropological and ethnological doctrines. This was true. My study endeavored to explore the universal foundation of Southwest Indian beliefs, finding parallels in Chinese Taoism and Tibetan Buddhism, and in the archetypal findings of Carl G. Jung. When I objected to the Press' rejection, we agreed to a compromise. The manuscript was to be submitted by the editorial board to an outside authority. If he approved it, the Press would publish it; if not, I would accept the Press' rejection. The authority chosen, unknown to me, was the most orthodox anthropologist in the country — Dr. Clyde Kluckhohn of the Department of Anthropology, Harvard University. He not only approved the book, but wrote the beautiful Foreword for it. The book was published in 1950 and has been reissued by other houses for thirty-five years, including a two-volume Japanese translation.

My next book on Indians was *Book of the Hopi*, published the following decade, in 1963. To write it, I lived nearly three years among the Hopis in Arizona. The book integrated for the first time their Creation Myth, the legends of their migrations, and the esoteric meanings of their annual nine religious ceremonials. These were freely given to me by some thirty kiva chiefs, clan leaders, and elders who wanted their tribal beliefs preserved for their children and grandchildren. I acknowledged them as the rightful authors by giving in the book their names, villages, clans, and religious society affiliations. Oswald Fredericks, or White Bear as he preferred to be called, acted as my interpreter and helped to gather the material. Publication was underwritten by the Charles Ulrick and Josephine Bay Foundation in New York.

The book presented the world view of the Hopi Traditionalists, those who upheld the ancient tribal beliefs. The Progressive or Tribal Council faction, dominated by the Bureau of Indian Affairs, considered this to be outmoded superstition which impeded Progress. Another division of opinion occurred in the Anglo world. Academic anthropologists and ethnologists refused to accept the book because the Hopi beliefs were founded on mysticism, not concrete fact. This objection by rational scientific observers had been voiced as far back as 1890 by the pioneer ethnologist Alexander M. Stephen, who first recorded the details of Hopi ceremonials. He stated that their ceremonialism was too abstract to understand, that it required a sixth sense of the Hopis themselves. The Western world still generally rejects anything that smacks of the rationally unknown, all that borders on the sixth-sense realm of mysticism. The Hopis, like all of Indian America, are polarized to the opposite side of our dual nature, to the realm of intuition, dreams and visions. One can't understand Indian ceremonialism unless he accepts their mode of thought. Despite the controversies about *Book of the Hopi*, it has been issued in innumerable editions, from mass paperbacks to foreign translations, during the last twenty-three years.

It is not strange that all my five books about Indians were flops at first and encountered opposition, gaining acceptance only years later. They ran against the tide of prejudice and mistrust of Indians. This general opinion has now changed. Native Americans, as they are now known, are accepted as an important segment of our national commonwealth, and they are enriching our life by writing about themselves. Yet my own books illustrate what I mean by saying a writer must often disregard what has been written and sink his roots deep into the land. And what is deeper than this great heartland of a continent and its indigenous people? The Hopi pueblo of Oraibi, dating from 1150 A.D., is the oldest continuously inhabited settlement in the United States; and ancient Pueblo Bonito in Chaco Canyon, the first prototypal city, the model for present Southwest architecture and great communal housing projects. Indian culture and religion have much to teach us. So much for sinking our roots into Indian America.

Now for the specific influences of past literature on one's own work. The literature of the Southwest is an older and richer lode of dramatic material than that of any other region. With the coming of the Spanish *conquistadores* in the sixteenth century began a rich accumulation of chronicles of exploration and discovery. Coronado's expedition of 1540, chronicled in Castañeda's *Relación de la Jornada de Cíbola*, and Marcos de Niza's *Descubrimiento de las Siete Ciudades* gave accounts of the search for the seven legendary Cities of Cíbola. They were followed by Villagra's epic poem celebrating the expeditions of Oñate, the accounts of exploratory travels by Espejo, Father Kino, Padre Garcés, and many others. Santa Fe, the first and oldest capital in the United States, was founded in 1610—before the Anglo Pilgrims landed at Plymouth Rock. The Spanish stamp on the land and the literature of the Southwest has never been erased. It differentiates us from all other regions.

Anglo dominance from the Atlantic to the Pacific reached the Southwest early in the nineteenth century. The Mountain Men, trappers and traders, penetrated the mountains and deserts. The exploits of Old Bill Williams, Kit Carson, and numerous others furnished tales still endlessly retold. Prospectors and the great gold rushes left more exciting literature, as did the covered wagon trains bringing the first American settlers on the heels of the last Indian wars.

Dramatic events succeeded one another swiftly. The war with Mexico resulted in the United States' annexation of all northern Mexico. During the American Civil War, Confederate troops briefly occupied part of the Southwest. The cowboy and the open range were replaced by the rancher and barbed wire, stage coaches by train and automobile. Before we realized it, detonation of the first atomic bomb near Alamogordo ushered in the Atomic Age, and the discovery of the richest uranium deposits in the world throughout the Southwest. Little cowtowns and mining camps mushroomed into cities. . . . And the changes are still taking place.

Historians haven't been able to record fully this fabulous era, it has unfolded so rapidly. Contemporary writers, however, are finding its dramatic events excellent subjects for novels, short stories and biographies. These, of course, further enrich our literature.

The westward expansion, however, also gave birth to a unique and resplendent American myth. A triumphant epic of conquest, the Winning of the West. Under the dictate of "Manifest Destiny," we exterminated beaver and buffalo, gutted the mountains for gold and silver, leveled whole forests under the axe, uprooted the grasslands. All who participated in this destructive March of Empire were automatically enhallowed as heroic characters in the operatic American Myth. Not only the petty criminal fleeing from a jail sentence, the ambitious land-grabber, the horse thief, became a noble pioneer settler, but soldiers like Custer and Chivington; a fictitious character created by a theatrical producer in New York and named Buffalo Bill; the young Bowery tough glorified as Billy the Kid; cattle barons and cattle rustlers; and gamblers; even the Two-Gun Man, the Killer, the Outlaw, applauded for his prowess.

The main theme of this fictitious victory of Good over Evil resulted in America's only true Morality Play—the Cowboy-Indian movie thriller, an indigenous art form as fundamental to America as the symphony and ballet to Europe. Its most popular form in literature is the phenomenal stock "Western."

Perhaps this species of writing was introduced, or at least first gained worldwide acceptance, by the novels of Zane Grey. I was addicted to them as a boy, and still think highly of them despite the low opinion held by literary scholars. Zane Grey's prototypal Westerns are indeed a lower form of literature, but their achievements rank high. They were not cheaply conceived, and they served as literature for a generation of children and grownups. They introduced the most significant and scenic locations in the Southwest to readers in America and abroad. And their characters acted the roles of archetypes unconsciously understood by everyone.

There is a great difference between them and the current flood of Western and Frontier paperbacks quickly concocted for immediate profit. These popular tales distort historical fact, make heroes out of cold-blooded killers in barroom brawls, and glorify young cattle drivers working for forty dollars a month and chuck as romantic Knights of the Golden West. Indians they portray as either savage Comanches or sentimental Red Brothers. Yet harshly as these pulp-paper yarns may be judged, they seem to fill the need of the immature for unthinking action and unrestrained violence.

We more mature writers of the New Southwest can't continue to indulge this fictional portrayal of the Old Southwest. If our writing is to hold water, we must discern the subjective and tragic truths behind our triumphant epic of conquest, the psychological compulsions that dominated us. We must delve deeper into a subject than it has been presented, try to find the reality behind the myth. Our views, being contrary to popular belief, may of course get us into hot water. As an example, I'd like to sketch very briefly my experience with one such book.

It began fifty years ago when I was living in Los Angeles. Visiting my mother and sister's family one afternoon, I met a little old lady familiarly known only as "Aunt Allie." She was dependent upon nearby relatives for bed and meals. Her only money came from peddling withered flowers from door to door. Full of colorful tales, she persuaded me to write her "life story" for the few dollars it might bring her.

I began jotting down her reminiscences. She had been born near Council Bluffs, Iowa. Orphaned as a child, she began waiting tables at the Planters House when she was sixteen. Here she met and married a young teamster named Virgil Earp. They made the overland trip by covered wagon to Tombstone, Arizona, where they joined Virgil's two brothers, Wyatt and Morgan. The "Fighting Earps of Tombstone," no less!

They had been made famous in 1931 by publication of Stuart N. Lake's biography, *Wyatt Earp, Frontier Marshal.* Allegedly dictated by Wyatt himself, it portrayed him as the West's greatest frontiersman and marshal, a model for movies and Westerns. A dashing single man, he was described as living in Tombstone's best hotel and helping to support his brothers' families by his lucrative gambling.

Aunt Allie derided the book as "a passel of lies." Actually, Wyatt was married to a girl named Mattie. All three Earp brothers and their wives lived in small adobes in the disreputable part of town shunned by respectable mining and business families. While the men were hunting jobs, Mattie and Aunt Allie supported them by taking in sewing. Soon they were joined by two more brothers, and all began to work as saloonkeepers, dealers, and gamblers. Then Virgil was elected town marshal.

Aunt Allie described Wyatt as a tinhorn gambler who associated with a gang of toughs and rustlers, neglected his wife Mattie, spent all his money on a traveling theatrical troupe member named Sadie, and got into trouble over the fight at the O.K. Corral. All the Earps left Tombstone in 1883, scarcely three years after they had arrived. Wyatt deserted his wife Mattie and went to San Francisco. Here he took up with Josie, Josephine Sarah Marcus, the young daughter of a wealthy Jewish merchant. They began living together and traveling around the country. Mattie, meanwhile, broke and friendless, wound up in another mining camp and committed suicide.

At this point in her narrative Aunt Allie refused to talk any more. I soon discovered why. Josie, Wyatt's common-law wife who had been living in Los Angeles since his death in 1929, had called on my mother and sister, threatening court action against me if I published Aunt Allie's story.

Aunt Allie's and Lake's versions were so contradictory I went to Arizona to research the historical facts. In Tucson the Arizona Pioneers Historical Society turned over to me its files of manuscripts, letters, and old newspapers. Then I went to Tombstone, consulting all available records and interviewing old residents. All this material documented Aunt Allie's account and revealed a sorry tale indeed of the five Earp brothers in Tombstone.

Jim was a saloonkeeper who lived in quiet obscurity. Youthful Warren became a stage driver and was shot and killed during a drunken brawl in a saloon. Morgan was a gambler. He was shot in the back and killed while playing pool in a saloon. Virgil, the most honest and courageous man of them all, was ambushed at night outside a saloon, shot and maimed. For the rest of his life he roamed the West with Aunt Allie, prospecting vainly for gold, and died unknown.

Wyatt was a supreme confidence man who had played many roles—church deacon, policeman, saloonkeeper, gambler, and bunco artist. A lifelong exhibitionist, ridiculed alike by his own family and the public press, he was run out of Arizona after the O.K. Corral killings, following President Chester A. Arthur's proclamation threatening to declare martial law if the Territory were not cleaned up. Only Wyatt reaped fame as America's greatest frontier marshal from Lake's book.

I summarized these facts in my book *The Colorado*, published in 1946. Believing that no one would be interested in the full story of this old Tombstone Travesty as I called it, I donated my long manuscript on the Earps to the Arizona Historical Society merely as a record for its files. Lake, however, threatened a lawsuit in the California civil court against the publishers, editor, and myself if I did not make public retraction of what I had written in *The Colorado*. This I refused to do, for while Lake's book largely comprised allegedly verbatim quotations from Wyatt, Lake in his letter to my publishers affirmed that Wyatt never dictated a word to him. Lake had met Wyatt only five months before Earp's death in 1929, when he was eighty years old, and he had died two years before Lake's book was published. Thus Lake admitted sole responsibility for the biography's fictitious contents. Nevertheless, one of his attorneys went to Tucson, reviewed my unpublished manuscript, then dropped the threatened suit.

I was content to drop the matter too. But more books and movies on the Fighting Earps came out, followed by a national TV series on Wyatt. A street in Dodge City was renamed after him, and a ship ploughing through Antarctic ice was christened the *Wyatt Earp*. Requests for my manuscript became so frequent that the secretary of the Historical Society suggested to me that it should be published.

Before doing so, I wanted to establish the time and place of Mattie's suicide. My friend John Gilchriese—who today has the largest collection of Earpiana—joined me in a 1,400-mile search through Arizona. We arrived in Florence one day in March, 1959, just before the Court House offices closed. An obliging records clerk allowed us to inspect some old documents just discovered in the basement. They were the handwritten records of the inquest held on the death of Mattie Earp. They revealed a tragic story. Deserted by Wyatt, and penniless, she had finally straggled into the mining camp of Pinal and become a prostitute. On July 2, 1888, she gave her last small breastpin to the last man to visit her, asking him to buy her some whiskey and laudanum to make her sleep. Next morning she was found dead, both bottles empty. Depositions were taken from three other men who had visited her. All testified that Mattie had told them her husband had left her and she didn't want to live any longer. Judge Benson, the coroner, wrote the cause of her death was suicide because her husband had deserted her and added that Wyatt Earp was a blackleg, a gambler, and a coward. Pinal, when John Gilchriese and I drove there, was a crumbled ghost town. The graveyard where Mattie had been buried was a mass of weeds, brush and cacti which had obliterated all grave markers.

Returning to Los Angeles, I told Aunt Allie of our findings and she finally revealed the skeleton in the Earp family closet. Josie Earp, the second wife, was the girl called "Sadie." At the age of twenty Josie had joined a traveling theatrical troupe which had played in Tombstone, where Wyatt had fallen in love with her and abandoned Mattie. This was why Josie had been afraid Aunt Allie's memoirs would reveal her former identity and the cause of Mattie's suicide and why Lake had denied her existence in Tombstone.

Aunt Allie then told me of more happenings in Tombstone. Of Wyatt's undercover activities as a member of a gang preying on the town. Of the innumerable town and mining properties he had bought, although he had no visible means of support. And that the splitting of the gang into two rival factions was the reason for the murders in the O.K. Corral. A sordid record indeed. . . .

In 1960 my *Earp Brothers of Tombstone*, based on Aunt Allie's narrative, was finally published—thirty years after I had begun it. It is still being reprinted as documented source material twenty-five years later. Yet other books and writers still deny its documented authenticity. Today, a century after the events took place, an ice cream parlor in Tombstone features a de luxe chocolate sundae called the "Wyatt Earp Special." A mural on the wall of the Pioneer Clothing Store shows his stalwart figure in frock coat, still keeping stern vigil over town. And at the annual Helldorado celebration there is re-enacted, in full costume, the "Fighting Earps" killing the "Cowboy Renegades" in the O.K. Corral, to the wild applause of thousands of visitors.

I have never considered my book on the Earps as simply the debunking of a biographer's book by another writer. Its purpose is far greater. The Winning of the West is still for most of us a myth impervious to harsh reality, a myth of the conquest of a great virgin land by a people wholly virtuous. Dedicated to material gain, we are still continuing our conquest by ruthless exploitation—destroying the land, polluting the air, contaminating all its surface waters, lowering the underground water levels, all decreasing to a dangerous degree the quality of human life.

The myth is still reflected in our obsession with the omnipotent dollar, economic and political corruption on all levels, and by the streak of violence imbedded in our nature as a people. What is the psychological source of these compulsive motivations?

There are many individuals and groups trying to discover what makes us what we are, trying to change our mode of thought, and halt this suicidal course. It is an uphill effort. But it will be worth continuing if we of the New Southwest can finally discover ourselves in our fictional beliefs about the Old Southwest. Only then will we achieve the plenitude and freedom promised by a great land and its earliest people. This is the challenge we writers face today.

BIBLIOGRAPHY OF SELECTED WORKS BY FRANK WATERS

The Man Who Killed the Deer. New York, Toronto: Farrar & Rinehart, Inc., 1941.

The Colorado. New York, Toronto: Rinehart & Company, Ind., Rivers of America Series, 1946.

Masked Gods: Navaho and Pueblo Ceremonialism. Albuquerque: The University of New Mexico Press, 1950.

The Earp Brothers of Tombstone. New York: Clarkson N. Potter, Inc., 1960.

Book of the Hopi. New York: The Viking Press, 1963.

Rolando Hinojosa-Smith, Ellen Clayton Garwood Centennial Professor of Creative Writing at the University of Texas, is the author of nine novels.

ROLANDO HINOJOSA-SMITH

THE OTHER
AMERICAN LITERATURES

In keeping with the general theme "Old Southwest/New Southwest: Personal Reflections," my remarks are titled *The Other American Literatures*. The emphasis will be on that American literature which most often presents a fusion of two cultures which were English and Spanish in origin.

I should like to open by saying that the literature we all write is American literature. It all begins with the early New Englanders, moves on to the fine Southern black and white writers, and in its westward movement, to Asian-American, other Black, along with Native American and Hispanic contributors. Ours is a large country, and its literature, then, is not relegated to that of our fellow citizens on the East Coast. Moreover, it has been an overall contribution that has made American literature richer than first envisioned by certain academics who, too early before adequate assessment could have been made, began to catalogue, to categorize, and to place much of American letters into neat little boxes from which they could then cull, sort, and prescribe what was and what was not American literature. Worse still, some began, willy-nilly, to tag with hyphens or with regional appellations whatever suited them at the time. One of the educational crimes is that some of those muddleheaded but convenient ideas were passed on to their undergraduate and junior graduate students.

In their penchant to simplify, they failed to notice that this American literature which is labeled with a hyphen or designated as

17

minority—and hence not-as-good—can't help but be American literature since we, all of us, write about American events, and principally, as most writers, we write about life in our native land. This last, the matter of our native land, is inescapable. Our characters' lives are carried out in a certain place, and, in the majority of cases, on American soil, an American place, an American region.

Therefore, one does not fly in the teeth of truth to say that it is *all* American literature. To deny it on emotional grounds is to fly in the face of available evidence. In brief, it does no good to label American literature under convenient sub-headings such as Black Literature, Asian-American Literature, and so on. You see, once one starts on that winding, hyphenated road, one is bound to run into all manner of roadblocks. For example, Jerzi Kosinski—Polish-born—writes here in the United States and may write in Polish, for all I know; or take the interesting case of Isaac Bashevis Singer, who writes in Polish and in Yiddish, but whose son usually translates his material for him; our own Hemingway who made much of his fame writing about American expatriates in Europe and Africa; or, in another artistic field, the Russian-born Irving Berlin who wrote *God Bless America* or the foreign-born George Gershwin who composed *An American in Paris* as well as an opera about a group of fellow Americans in South Carolina. One can go on to mention Canadian-born Saul Bellow and two descendants of Eastern European immigrants, Joseph Heller and Philip Roth, and so on. Now, do these two produce "American Jewish literature?" I know they don't, and you do, too; nor do we even consider them in those lights. Still, the relationships they commonly describe are certainly Jewish for the most part.

But if we so labeled them, the voices of protestation would be heard long and loudly, too. They write American literature, don't they? Well, so do those writers whom we capriciously and conveniently designate as minority writers. I'll mention but three at this time: Frank Chin, Ishmael Reed, and Wendy Rose, all three of the Bay Area. Chances are very good that all three carry the hyphenated label because of their small press background. I'll come back to small presses in a moment.

It is also a truth that our larger publishing houses will continue to make these distinctions as long as the readers let them, as long as teachers go along and let them, and perhaps until someone hits them with a two-by-four to get their attention. It's as simple and as complex as that.

How did most of these distinctions and designations come about? I suppose it started with the academic contretemps suffered by William

Lyon Phelps when he was an Assistant Professor at Harvard in 1896.
In the fall of that year, he introduced a course which he called American
Literature. He chose the following writers: Hawthorne, Poe, Melville,
Whitman, and Dickinson. The following semester, he was threatened
with dismissal if he persisted in teaching that "so-called American
Literature." He desisted, of course, but this in part led to the
strengthening of the Modern Language Association of America later
on. From the preceding, you must also appreciate that early American
literature—that of the New Englanders I mentioned—had a difficult
time competing with British writing at the beginning. And, in our own
universities, American literature had an agonizing battle trying to get
through the entrenched university curriculum committees. The first
doctorate in American literature, by the way is a twentieth-century
phenomenon.

True, we're now eighty-six years into the century, but it wasn't
until after World War II that universities in the American heartland—
the University of Kansas, for one, and the University of Missouri, for
another—began to offer serious, programmatic, and systematic courses
of study in American literature leading toward the earning of senior
degrees.

Knowing this, then, it is easier to understand—if not accept nor
agree with—the hard time faced by the other and often omitted
contributions to American literature later on. All manner of
opposition, some of it quite resolute, came about; this, too, is no
different from that faced by United States Western writers until they
established their own organizations and associations and until some of
them became subjects of serious study by interested academics in the
Modern Language Association. It must be said that the writers were
going to continue writing whether or not they were recognized by any
organized body.

As a parenthesis, I must say that the M.L.A., the Modern Language
Association, more than any other nationally organized professional
association, has done more for the enlarging of American literature
with membership, money, and good will. Please remember I am
speaking of the national body, not the regional M.L.A.'s.

My experience with regional M.L.A.'s has been an educational one:
they are unusually hidebound when compared to the national parent.
You may think it ungracious of me to mention those regional
organizations since they aren't represented here today, but I happen to
belong to one of them, the South Central M.L.A. And, I'll tell you a
story: around 1971 or so, I wrote to Louis Kampf of M.I.T. who, through

his office as President of the national M.L.A., extended invitations to those unrepresented literatures to participate in the organization. I wrote him a nice, short letter and he answered willingly, putting his money where his mouth was, as it were. At the same time, I tried to propose a panel and some papers on Chicano literature at a regional M.L.A. Well! I had to go through a number of obstacles such as getting up lists of names and who-knows-what-all. This, of course, is no different from any other petition, but since the national entity had extended the invitation, I, foolishly as it turned out, thought it would apply to the regional level.

I chose not to follow the regional route. By not doing so, Chicano literature or Mexican American literature, as it has been variously called, was represented on panels, forums, and in the presentation of formal papers on the national level years before the regional M.L.A.'s decided to recognize what it was we were doing in this contemporary American literary field. Chances are you are thinking that I am blowing off some pent-up steam and bile, but nothing could be farther from my mind. I neither become angry nor do I get even, as the saying goes. If anything, I usually get busy remedying the cure.

But—you may ask—didn't M.L.A. have to be educated about other American literatures? Yes. How? By receiving evidential proof of worthy publications, papers, readings, and such. The times were ripe, someone will say, and I will agree. But then, you must also agree with me that people make the times and the events which will lead us right back to the labelings and to the difficulties first faced by William Lyon Phelps in the heart and soul of New England.

Now, given the feistiness, pugnacity, and yes, the truculence of those who had been omitted, it was understandably human for many Blacks, Asian Americans, Native American Indians, and others to have carved out a territory at the beginning. Some of the positions taken were incorrect, to put it at its mildest. Others were off target, to put it baldly. For instance, it was claimed that no one else could write and publish literary criticism or creative literature in those fields other than Blacks, Chicanos, etcetera. The touchiness was also understandable at that time, but it shouldn't be so now, although some people, we must admit, never get the word. This last, of course, includes us all: writers, teachers, students, the general populace, and last, as usual, the publishers and their agents who try to buy us off with a lunch or a dinner or a drink to buy their inventoried stock. Hardly a serious relationship, this last.

In the '60's, the larger publishing houses set about establishing their own market in this newly recognized literature. There were several errors committed by them, and I will touch on one: they rushed to publish what was available then and what was becoming available; in this rush, they published much of the bombast and welter that was foisted on them. And, in this rush—since they misjudged and thought this American literature to be regional and transitory—they got in, made scads of money, and then got out. One of the many phenomena of the '60's was that the smaller presses came into their own again as they had in the '20's and '30's; but now, they did so with a vengeance. Many made plans to work their way into the academy, not as university presses, but rather as presses parallel to the university ones. Many of us know of the death and disappearance of many university presses in the '60's and '70's.

I'll now stop for another parenthetical remark: Simon and Schuster was a small press at one time. Its fortune was established through the publication of crossword puzzles and the like. Small presses today, and this is not idle speculation, are being eyed with interest by the larger publishing houses, as they should, since some of the small presses are very good indeed. And now that the market analysts of the major houses have shown that the expansion of American literature in the '60's was not a flower child's delusion but rather a rock-hard truth, sensible men and women are turning their corporate Eastern eyes west of the Hudson River as well. This vision will be another step in the widening of the vision and scope of American literature.

This will be a beginning of a new relationship. A serious, meaningful event on American soil, by American participants.

You have every right to wonder if I'm sticking my neck out by these prognostications. Let me assure you that I'm not: there exist nationally published words about these coming events in no less a publication than the *New York Times Review of Books*. Those folks, as we say in the South, usually know what they're talking about.

The current major publishing houses have just about written off the university presses because of the latter's apparent and often evident immutability. But the university presses will also change in time. If not, they'll die in the academic marketplace and deservedly so.

Not all, and not the majority either, of the previously ignored American literature deserves publication: there aren't enough trees in the American forests for that. However, much *is* being published. And much which will be written will deserve close reading and assessment and eventual publication. Its durability belongs to time, to what Lionel Trilling, when he spoke of money, once called the great leveller. Time has always been on the side of those who use it wisely; we'll now see, in time, what this American literature with its new relationships accomplishes by the end of the century.

And, since my time does not permit a complete recounting of all the ignored American literature I've been speaking of, I'll concentrate on the primarily Southwestern contribution of those Spanish and English origins I mentioned at the top of my remarks.

When the descendants of the old Spanish and Mexican settlers became American citizens either immediately or one year after the proclamation of the Treaty of Guadalupe Hidalgo, this marked the beginning of the newest contribution to American letters. Almost all of this newer American work was in Spanish, and historical reasons certainly abound for this phenomenon. As time goes on in that century, the Spanish language contribution continues, but English also makes its presence known, particularly in the territory of New Mexico, as studies by Doris Meyer of Brooklyn College pointed out.[1] In Texas, for another example, the Lozano family of San Antonio maintained a healthy Hispanic contribution to American letters with their publication of *La Prensa*, a daily newspaper shipped by rail to subscribers throughout the state for over half a century, from 1912 to the early 1960's.

In passing, it isn't surprising that the appearance of writing by American citizens in Texas of Mexican descent was in Spanish. Nor, with its late entry to the Union, that in sparsely populated New Mexico, given its educational background of Catholic nuns serving as public school teachers, that English would predominate in the contribution of writers of Mexican descent. California, with all of its variety, presented literature in both languages, but the tendency, in keeping with its rapid urbanization after World War II, pointed to a decided output in English.

In Texas, however, traditionally a conservative and predominantly rural state, Spanish was retained not only in oral knowledge, but also in the written form. *La Prensa* helped, of course, but so did the Mexican schools operated in South Texas and in the Rio Grande Valley next to the Gulf. English contributions existed, to be sure, but it is no accident that both men and women writers were, and continue to be, at home in both languages. The poetry by Angela de Hoyos, for one example, can be read in English and in Spanish. Those with a dual knowledge of both languages and cultures can enjoy the mixture in de Hoyos's poetry.[2] She is not alone in this, of course; one must also point to the Texan Evangelina Vigil and to another fellow San Antonian, Carmen Tafolla.[3] All three are equally adept in one language or the other. These are but three poets. In the narrative prose work, Tomás Rivera's *...y no* *se lo tragó la tierra* set the early mark for this American literature in the Spanish language. The novel, despite its bloodless translation into English, has seen over seven printings in the last fifteen years.[4] My own work has seen various levels and degrees of language usage: Spanish, English, and in one work in a blend of both to reveal the amalgamation of the culture peculiar to the Rio Grande Valley.[5]

For some ten years, assorted readers have asked what this literature was, and why was it written in Spanish at times, and whom did it address. The more knowing of readers, by their lights at least, asked if the themes were universal. This American literature was subjected to the same questioning as was that of those unacceptable writers William Lyons Phelps introduced in Harvard in that fall of 1896.

One had to be very patient in those days, but one also had to keep an eye on those who wished to exclude this, as other American literatures, from what they considered to be the true American literature. Aesthetics were missing, they said. It was strictly utilitarian, they said. And what is this literature, anyway? Is there such a thing? And on, and on. But Time was there, and in time they gave up. Whether they gave up willingly or not is not a matter of importance, nor should it be. This part of our American literature has other immediate concerns: a continuity; the establishment of a body of literary criticism based not on friendships or tendentiousness, but on sound, basic criticism of every stripe; and the continued use of whatever language the poets and prose writers contribute.

As always, it will be years before everybody gets the word, but the assigning of this or that corner of American literature to the Chicano literature I've been speaking of today is as incorrect as the stance of that Dean at Harvard who was wrong at the top of his voice some ninety years ago. He should have remembered that poor literature is marked down by time and history, that the literature which endures does so by its own merits. And that conferences, symposia, and meetings such as this one shared by all of us may serve as prima-facie evidence, but eventually as best evidence, regarding the rude health of American literature as we know it today.

ENDNOTES

I should like to thank the Tucsonans and the personnel of the Tucson Public Library, and Judy Lensink, the Project Director for this important conference and gathering. I cannot nor will I omit David Laird, Librarian for the University of Arizona, and Tom Phelps of NEH who has served as Program Officer for over a hundred projects in libraries nationwide. Conferences such as these take on all manner of organization and coordination, and we, the participants, usually take what glory there is by being on center stage. One of the points of my opening remarks is to show that my life as an academician and writer has not come about on my own: many people worked toward this life of mine as hard as the ones responsible for our conference entitled OLD SOUTHWEST/NEW SOUTHWEST.

[1]Doris Meyer, "Anonymous Poetry in Spanish-language New Mexico Newspapers, 1880-1890," *Bilingual Review/Revista Bilingüe*, 2 and 3 (September-October, 1975), pp. 259-275; Angela de Hoyos, *Woman, Woman* (Houston: Arte Público Press, 1985).

[3]Evangelina Vigil, ed., *Woman of Her Word: Hispanic Women Write* (Houston: Arte Público Press, 1984); Carmen Tafolla, *Curandera*, (San Antonio: M & A Editions, 1983).

[4]Tomás Rivera, *...y no se lo tragó la tierra* (Berkeley: Quinto Sol Publications, 1971).

[5]See, Rolando Hinojosa-Smith, *Estampas del Valle y Otras Obras* (Berkeley: Quinto Sol, 1973); Hinojosa-Smith, *Korean Love Songs* (Berkeley: Editorial Justa Publications, 1978); Hinojosa-Smith, *Klail City und Umgebung*, trans. by Yolanda Julia Broyles (Frankfurt, Germany: Suhrkamp, 1981); Hinojosa-Smith, "The Valley," *Bilingual Review/Revista Bilingüe* (Ypsilanti, Michigan: Eastern Michigan University, 1983); Hinojosa-Smith, *Dear Rafe* (Houston: Arte Público Press, 1985).

ARRELL MORGAN GIBSON

THE AUTHOR AS IMAGE MAKER FOR THE SOUTHWEST

The Southwest is a land of variant, captivating landscapes, many charming, creative, contrasting cultures, and peoples sustained by an anomalous and intriguing heritage. Viewpoints differ as to its dimensions, its geographic extent, its boundaries. Prehistoric, historic, and contemporary components, as well as a rather common environmental base, fuse this quadrant of the United States into an integrated identifiable region: the Southwest consists of a heartland, Arizona and New Mexico, flanked by the rimlands of California, Texas and Oklahoma. And the Southwest is a land of changing images; at times it has been held in low esteem, at others in high esteem, from extremes of scorn and rejection to respect, even affectionate embrace.

These shifting images have been formed largely from the writings of authors who have published their perceptions of the Southwest as exotic environment, their estimate of it as a habitation site for fellow citizens. No other region of the United States has been the subject of such extended and contradictory literary and partisan attention. Certainly no other region's image has been so sensitive, so responsive, to the author's published descriptions, judgment, and assessments.

The earliest known published appraisals of this region were written by Spaniards, either as resident muses imagining from afar the nature of this land and its people, or by immigrants to New Spain. Iberian colonials were struck by the Southwest's vastness, its contrasting environments, its prospects for spiritual harvest among native peoples for the Holy See, its promise of fortunes in gold and silver for king and conquistadore, and the *simpático* similarity of many of its parts to their beloved homeland. It is important to bear in mind that the Hispanic perception of the Southwest was derived from the flow of Iberian colonists migrating on a south-to-north axis from Mexico to this northern frontier of New Spain, in contrast to the traditional Anglo-American continental thrust on an east-west concourse from the Atlantic shore into the Pacific Basin.

Garci Rodríguez Ordóñez de Montalvo was the first writer to describe the Southwest. He conjured *Las Sergas de Esplandían*, an essay, clearly the issue of an over-stimulated imagination, that depicted a mythical land called California, calculated to arouse the adventure lust and sensual imperative of readers. *Las Sergas* reports that "on the right hand of the Indies," there is a treasure-rich island "called California very close to the Terrestrial Paradise," which is populated by women who live "in the fashion of Amazons . . . strong and hardy of bodies, of ardent courage and great force." Ruler of California is Queen Calafia, "very large in person, the most beautiful of them all, of blooming years . . . strong of limb and of great courage, more than any of those who had filled her throne before her . . . and in her thoughts desirous of achieving great things."[1]

Reports of mythical centers of dazzling beauty and wealth situated in New Spain's northern territory—Seven Cities of Cibola, Cale, Tierra de las Perlas, and the Gran Quivira—joined the *Las Sergas* fable to form, in the impressionable sixteenth-century Hispanic mind, believable lures for adventure, fortune, and fame. The Seven Cities of Cibola was described as an incomparable El Dorado, its outer walls constructed of gold, the doors of houses and shops covered with turquoise, green like a forest. Cale, Tierra de las Perlas, was depicted as a nation where the plaza of each of its towns was marked by a tall mound of the purest pearls. And Gran Quivira was rated the richest center on the northern frontier, where women served their men from golden pitchers, tiny golden bells affixed to branches of shade trees tinkled in the soft breeze, and even Quiviran children wore gold bracelets on their wrists and ankles. Writings transmitting these myths to generations of Spaniards included Fray Marcos' *Report*, and Pedro Castañeda's *The Coronado Expedition*.[2]

These fantasy impressions were challenged by the Anglo-American advent. Yankees were latecomers to the Southwest, during the 1790's, probing its eastern margins from their settlements in the lower

Arrell Morgan "Luke" Gibson, Professor of History at the University of Oklahoma, has written twenty-three books and over 150 essays on the Southwest.

Mississippi Valley, its western margins from aboard their fleets of Pacific-based whaler and trader ships.

The earliest and most influential writings by Americans pertaining to the Southwest were Zebulon Montgomery Pike's *Explorations and Travels Through Territories of North America*, William Shaler's *Journal of a Voyage Between China and the Northwestern Coast of North America*, and Edwin James' *Account of an Expedition from Pittsburgh to the Rocky Mountains*. Pike and James described the Southwest's heartland, Shaler commented on the Southwest's Pacific rimland.[3]

During 1806 the Secretary of War placed Captain Pike in command of an expedition with orders to explore, map and describe a large portion of the Trans-Missouri territory to provide federal officials essential knowledge of what they had acquired by the recent Louisiana Purchase Treaty. Arriving at the Great Bend of the Arkansas River, Pike detached a segment of his column, commanded by Lt. James Wilkinson, with orders to trace that stream to its mouth. Pike and his reduced column proceeded to the central Rocky Mountain region where they were arrested by a Spanish patrol up from Santa Fe and were detained in the Spanish settlements for several months before being permitted to return to the United States. Pike's published description of New Mexico and the West Texas portion of the Southwest was consistently negative. He regarded this region as a wasteland, unfit for most American pursuits. Pike did acknowledge the prospect of profitable trade for American merchants in the goods-starved Rio Grande settlements, should the Spanish government relax its ban on commerce with aliens. Wilkinson's memoir of his riverine reconnaissance, published as an addendum to Pike's journal, is descriptive of the Southwest's margins along the Arkansas River, and is scarcely favorable, his perceptions certainly conditioned by hardships he and his men suffered descending the ice-choked stream in crude pirogues and bull boats.

Shaler, a maritime trader, was primarily interested in the Southwest's commercial prospects. His observations of the Pacific rimland are less melancholy than those of Pike and Long. And *Journal of a Voyage* is not a regional libel, as are *Explorations and Travels* and *Account of an Expedition*.

The Stephen H. Long journal, kept by expedition scientist Edwin James, traces that exploring column in its peregrinations during 1819 and 1820 from the American settlements into the central Rocky Mountains, thence southward into eastern New Mexico in search of the headwaters of Red River, anticipated by federal officials to be the likely boundary separating United States and Spanish territory in the Southwest acceptable to Spanish negotiators. In the course of reconnoitering eastern New Mexico, Long chose a stream bed he determined to be the upper waters of Red River and followed its eastward course into the Texas panhandle and across Indian Territory (the future Oklahoma) to a point where that stream joined the Arkansas. It was only then that he became aware that he had followed the Canadian River, its course several hundred miles north of Red River. Long's reconnaissance of this portion of the Southwest was completed in the scorching heat of late summer and the expedition journal reflects his low opinion of the region—this great arid expanse "was providentially placed to keep the American people from ruinous diffusion." Long declared, "We have little apprehension of giving too unfavorable an account of this portion of the country. Though the soil is in some places fertile, the want of timber, of navigable streams, and water for the necessities of life, render it unfit residence for any but a nomad population. The traveller who shall any time have traversed its desolate sands, will, we think, join us in the wish that the region may forever remain the unmolested haunt of the native hunter, the bison, and the jackall [coyote]."[4]

The Pike and Long books, which characterized the Southwest as the "Great American Desert," and forged foundations for a regional image which survived into the twentieth century, caused the Southwest to be dismissed as a marginal land of only limited value to the national life. Nineteenth-century American society was predominantly agrarian; eighty to ninety percent of the population was rural, with most country-dwellers engaged in some form of agriculture. This economic fixation had evolved from early colonial times in the East and the Mississippi Valley environment of temperate climate with adequate rainfall to sustain crops without irrigation, the land timbered or prairie, based in rich loamy soils. Their agrarian preoccupation caused nineteenth-century Yankees to judge a territory by its agricultural prospects. Thus, those who read descriptions of the Southwest or who passed over it ratified Pike's and Long's scornful judgment of it.

Political leaders concluded that, inasmuch as the Southwest had been judged unfit for the dominant plowman's use, and no other discernible private use had surfaced there to attract private citizen investment and exploitation attention, they would convert it to the public purpose, to use it as a national territory, a decision which determined its fate for generations. Defining it as a military frontier, the

Secretary of War would concentrate there the nation's fortifications and communications facing first, Spanish, and later, Mexican, territories on the Southwestern border.

An additional function as a national territory would be for the Southwest to serve as a refuge for colonizing Indian nations residing in those portions of the United States on lands coveted by the "Great Land Animal," the pioneer settler. Federal officials reasoned that once ensconced on reservations in the Great American Desert, Indian nations would never again be faced with removal because the lands to be assigned to them in the Indian Territory were rated unfit for the civilized pursuits of American citizens. Eventually federal officials colonized sixty-seven different tribes in the so-called Indian Territory, situated on the Southwest's northeastern rim.

Even after the Mexican War (1846-1848) when, by the Treaty of Guadalupe-Hildago, Mexico ceded to the United States that portion of the Southwest beyond Indian Territory and Texas, the federal intent was to continue to use the enlarged Southwest as a national territory, additionally concentrating Indian nations therein, and enlarging the military defense area facing Mexico as required. National leaders assigned the Southwest the additional function of serving the nation as geographic connective tissue, as a vast land bridge, linking the Mississippi Valley and the Pacific shore with an all-weather passage for constructing the projected transcontinental railway. This would provide the United States a window on the Pacific and a strategic maritime connection for consummating Senator Thomas Hart Benton's dream of an abbreviated "Road to India."[5]

The half century after the Mexican War was a time when the Southwest's literary-initiated Great American Desert libel was joined by additional pejoratives—The Anglo El Dorado, a Violent Land, Pariah's Refuge, and America's Barrio. These provided writers for Beadle and Adams Company, dime novel and pioneer pulps publishers, prospectus writers, publicists, and promoters a virtually infinite range of subject matter.

The discovery of gold in the California Sierras during 1848 set off a region-wide feverish quest by rapacious fortune-seeking intruders. In less than a half a century they plundered the Southwest's prodigal natural bounty—precious and base minerals, fossil fuels, forests, and wildlife—mindlessly destroying, creating irreclaimable wastelands, vandalizing incomparable landscapes. The spoilers' unwarranted assumption that its natural resources were infinite abetted the inclination to assign to the Southwest a colonial-type role in the national life, that of humble supplier of essentials for sustaining the more advanced Eastern industrial establishment.

The image of Violent Land grew out of the Southwest becoming, after 1848, an arena for action, high-risk adventure, and frequent bloodletting. Its roots derive from the Mexican War; much of this land came under American dominion as a prize of conquest, by the triumph of American arms. Its violence additives include the Indian barrier, comprised of swift-riding Kiowa and Comanche raiders who made the Southern Plains a scalp alley for those daring to venture a passage through their territory. This hazard persisted until massed United States cavalry and infantry conquered these native terrors of the Southwest during the Red River War and forced their capitulation in 1874. And beyond, in southern New Mexico and Arizona, was the domain of the fierce Mimbreño and Chiricahua Apaches, led by Mangas Coloradas, Cochise, Victorio, Nana, and finally Geronimo. These Apaches resisted Anglo intruders until finally sustained campaigning by the United States Army forced Geronimo to capitulate in 1886.

The saga of the six-gun additionally embellished this image of Violent Land. Belle Starr, the Cherokee Kid and Ned Christie in anarchic postwar Indian Territory, and Billy the Kid, John Wesley Hardin, and Wyatt Earp in the heartland were notorious for their contempt for law and order. They supplied authors a half-century access to the mother lode of desperate, bloody, violent action literary themes. In this context, Owen Wister and Zane Grey immortalized the cowboy. His reckless adventures, from the ranches of the Cherokee Strip Livestock Association domain in Indian Territory to the mountain and desert ranges of New Mexico and Arizona, transmitted in books and pulps, titillated the reading public's vicarious quest for deadly adventure and fueled the Southwest image of Violent Land.

Easterners extended their scorn for the land to its people. In their ethnocentric view, the Southwest was populated largely by threateningly unlike peoples—Hispanics, Mestizos, and Indians. Their bigoted judgment caused them to assign to Southwestern peoples the inferior status of vassals, drawers of water and hewers of wood, worthy only of serf-like status to labor in the region's mines and forests, to draw the riches of nature's bounty from this land, and to build the railroads to transport these raw essentials to advanced communities in the eastern United States.

Assignment of Southwesterners to this inferior context was used as additional justification for designating the Southwest a colonial territory, a national outback, its people unworthy of reception into the

American community. Thus, the Southwest became a land of arrested political development, held in territorial status, dominated by marginal leadership. Also it became the habitat of castoffs and adventurers and a burying ground for political misfits from Washington, D.C. So-called "carpetbag" rule was a common and sustained phenomenon through much of the Southwest. Virtually all officials in a territorial government were appointed by the President and only limited self-determination was permitted residents of a territory as compared to residents of a state. Authors and orators, particularly those with business and political connections, in their writings and speeches maintained the image of unworthiness. The utterances of one national leader will suffice to illustrate the position of those committed to holding the Southwest in secondary status. Senator Albert Beveridge of Indiana, Chairman of the powerful United States Senate Committee on Territories, held up Indian Territory (future Oklahoma) statehood until 1907 because it was populated with a large proportion of unlike peoples, Native Americans. And his obsessive bigotry was responsible for New Mexico and Arizona being held on the threshold of the American Union until 1912, the last of the contiguous territories to be admitted to the Union. Beveridge's writings, largely articles in national magazines, and his speeches on the floor of the Senate and before public gatherings, were seasoned with vile references to the Southwest heartland—a community of "backward areas," each "stifled by their Spanish heritage," — "not equal in intellect, resources or population to the other states in the Union," their principal handicap that they were not "sufficiently American in their habits and customs."[6]

Not all Americans disdained the Southwest, however. During the 1840's and 1850's many Americans—soldiers, government officials, fortune seekers, and restless, curious adventurers—were drawn to the Southwest. Several, after viewing the land and its people, disputed the near-universally accepted regional slander, and a few published challenging counterstatements. They saw in the Southwest incomparable beauty, they detected an exotic charm in its people, and they were excited that here was a land populated by persons who practiced a different, yet attractive lifestyle, which rather than threatening them, drew them to it. Among these writings which sought to create a positive image for the Southwest were Josiah Gregg's *Commerce of the Prairies*, a commentary on Anglo-American trade opportunities in the Rio Grande settlements and a favorable report on the Hispanic population; George Ruxton's *Life in the Far West*, a report of his adventures and impressions in the upper reaches of the Southwest's heartland; Lewis

Garrard's *Wah-to-Yah and the Taos Trail*, a litany of delight yielded by the land and people of New Mexico to this young advocate of the Southwest; and John C. Fremont's *Report of the Exploring Expedition . . . California in the Years 1843-44*, in which the Great Pathfinder revealed his dream of the Great American Desert becoming a garden. As an officer of the United States Army commanding an expedition on orders to explore, map, and describe portions of the Southwest, he wrote warm comments on behalf of the region that provided an official challenge to the negative evaluations published by Pike and Long.

Another partisan of the Southwest was W.H.H. Davis, who served in the territorial government of New Mexico soon after the conquest. He wrote in *El Gringo: New Mexico and Her People* that, "Here a person experienced different feelings than when confined within cities . . . . He appears to breathe deeper, and to increase in stature; the sky seems blue and cleaner, the air purer, and the sun to shine more brightly." And "in beholding Nature's works" here "a man cannot fail to be better and wiser. Health seems to be the natural condition of man instead of disease, and a larger number of our persons live to a great old age than in any other part of our country."[7]

This trend of challenge to negative images continued after the Civil War. Two nonpareil statements published between 1865 and 1900 which influenced the attitudes of many American readers toward the Southwest were *The Delight Makers* issued in 1890 and *Land of Poco Tiempo* appearing in 1893. Adolph Bandelier, an archaeologist working the paleo-Indian ruins of northern New Mexico, composed in *The Delight Makers* a charming reconstruction of prehistoric culture in the Southwest centering on the ancestors of the modern Pueblo Indians. Charles F. Lummis, who became the late nineteenth century's premier publicist for the Southwest, expressed in *Land of Poco Tiempo* his admiration for its anomalous environment and pluralistic cultures. It became a classic study of the ambience and mystique of land and people in the Southwestern quadrant of the United States.

Regional image alteration received the very special attention of literary and art muses who settled in several colonies across the Southwest, principally at Carmel in California and Santa Fe and Taos in New Mexico. These aesthetic colonies flourished between 1900 and 1942. Painters in these refuges rendered countless canvases portraying the Southwest's exquisite landscapes, portraits of multi-ethnic peoples, amid scintillating lifestyles and village scenes. These paintings were exhibited widely across the United States and in Europe; many appeared in galleries, museums, and private collections. Certainly these works of art created a sympathetic attitude on the part of viewers toward the region's human and environmental subjects.[8]

However, writers resident in these colonies exercised an even greater influence in altering attitudes toward the Southwest and in the process improving its image. Their challenge to the near-indelible external perception of desert, violence, and general unworthiness, their advocacy of the Southwest and its people as a region and community worthy of respect and acceptance in the national life, had gradual but eventually considerable impact on reader attitudes. These included Alice Corbin Henderson (*The Penitentes*), Lynn Riggs (*Green Grow the Lilacs*), D.H. Lawrence (*The Plumed Serpent*), Robinson Jeffers (*Selected Poetry of Robinson Jeffers*), Mabel Dodge Luhan (*Winter in Taos*), Witter Bynner (*Red Rust*), Haniel Long (*Piñon Land*), Ben Botkin (*Folksay*), Oliver LaFarge (*Laughing Boy*), Willa Cather (*Death Comes for the Archbishop*), and above all of the colony-based literati — Mary Austin. Called "God's mother-in-law" by her writer associates because of her peremptory sense of community guardianship and obsessive but tolerated direction of the lives of others, Mary Austin cast a literary spell over indifferent and doubting Americans and generated by her writings a broadened national interest in the region. She became the pre-eminent publicist for the Southwest after Charles F. Lummis. She produced several books and countless essays and articles for popular magazines illuminating the region's environment, edifying its singular heritage, its tricultural society, and its prospects in the life of the nation. None of Austin's writings on the Southwest surpassed in quality and force her first book — *Land of Little Rain*. The collective alterative influence of the muse colonies in image transformation and change in external attitude was immense. In a very real sense the writers and artists residing in the Santa Fe, Taos, and Carmel colonies set the stage for a regional revolution.

Soon after the beginning of World War II, President Franklin D. Roosevelt ordered the placement of many war production enterprises and research compounds in the vast, sparsely settled Southwest. This precipitated an industrial, technological, and demographic revolution which spread in reverberating, expanding circles in space and time to touch every nook and cranny of this once nearly empty land. Immigrants manning this region-wide cluster of hi-tech enterprises found that the once scorned Southwest, with special applications, could be transformed into an environment where quality of life was achievable. These applications, of course, were technological elements applied to environmental alteration, devoted largely to the production of kilowatts and delivery of water. Thus, the nation's perception of the Southwest has shifted from wasteland to a new frontier where one may find the good life. The energy shortfall of the 1970's further improved the status of the Southwest in the national viewpoint—the Great American Desert became the Sun Belt, the nation's great settlement reserve for refugees from the Frost Belt.

Authors have not been indifferent to these developments. Just as their writings improved the Southwest's image, many now are on another track, seeking to create even another image for the region. They behold the phenomenal population surge into this Sun Belt. They are sensitized to the burden this places on the Southwest's limited resources. They witness the threat of invasive technology required to sustain this burgeoning population on the delicate environment. And they have turned their literary attention to the unique beauty of this milieu, stressing its fragile nature, seeking to build respect for it, and publicizing the threat that this industrial-demographic revolution poses to the region's environmental well-being. Their books, articles, and essays stress the limits of regional accommodation. Joseph Wood Krutch (*The Desert Year*) and Ann Woodin (*Home is the Desert*) portray the region's natural charm and its fragility. Philip Fradkin (*A River No More*) and Amadeo Rea, Peter Wiley and Robert Gottlieb (*Empires in the Sun*) calculate the limits to regional development. The goals of the modern school of writers on the Southwest are to build respect for the region and its natural and human resources, and to persuade the escalating population to so order their lives that they live in harmony with its unyielding imperatives.

ENDNOTES

[1]Garci Rodríguez Ordóñez de Montalvo, "Las Sergas de Esplandián," trans. Edward Everett Hale, *The Atlantic Monthly*, 82 (March, 1864), pp. 266-67.

[2]See *Narratives of the Coronado Expedition, 1540-1542*, George P. Hammond, and Agapito Rey, eds. (Albuquerque: University of New Mexico Press, 1940).

[3]See Zebulon Montgomery Pike, *The Expedition of Zebulon Montgomery Pike*, ed., Elliott Coues (New York: Francis P. Harper, 1895), 2 vols.; Edwin James, *Account of an Expedition from Pittsburgh to the Rocky Mountains, 1819-1820* in *Early Western Travels, 1748-1865*, ed.

Reuben G. Twaites (Cleveland: Arthur H. Clark Co., 1905); and William Shaler, *Journal of a Voyage from China to the Northwestern Coast of America Made in 1804* (Claremont, California: Saunders Studio Press, 1935).

[4]James, *Account of an Expedition*, p. 174.

[5]See Thomas Hart Benton, *Thirty Years' View of a History of the Working of the American Government for Thirty Years, from 1820 to 1850* (New York: Kasper and Horton, 1854), 2 vols.

[6]Howard R. Lamar, *The Far Southwest, 1846-1912* (New Haven: Yale University Press, 1966), p. 17; and Arrell Morgan

Gibson, *The West in the Life of the Nation* (Lexington: D.C. Heath Co., 1976), pp. 508-12.

[7]See Billy M. Jones, *Health-Seekers in the Southwest, 1817-1900* (Norman: University of Oklahoma Press, 1967), p. 87.

[8]See Arrell Morgan Gibson, *The Santa Fe and Taos Colonies: Age of the Muses, 1900-1942* (Norman: University of Oklahoma Press, 1983).

BIBLIOGRAPHY

Austin, Mary. *Land of Little Rain*. New York: Ballantine Books, 1971.

Ballard, Steven C., et al. *Water and Western Energy: Impacts, Issues, and Choices*. Boulder: Westview Press, 1982.

Bandelier, Adolph. *The Delight Makers*. New York: Dodd, Mead & Co., 1890.

Benton, Thomas Hart. *Thirty Years' View or a History of the Working of the American Government for Thirty Years, from 1820-1850*. New York: Kasper and Benton, 1854, 2 vols.

Botkin, Ben. *Folksay*. Norman: University of Oklahoma Press, 1931.

Bynner, Witter. *Red Rust*. Santa Fe: Rydal Press, 1942.

Cather, Willa. *Death Comes for the Archbishop*. New York: Alfred Knopf, 1927.

Davis, W.H.H. *El Gringo: New Mexico and Her People*. New York: Harper and Brothers, 1857.

Fradkin, Philip L. *A River No More: The Colorado River and the West*. Tucson: University of Arizona Press, 1984.

Fremont, John C. *Report of the Exploring Expedition to . . . California in the Years 1843-44*. Washington: Gales and Seaton, 1845.

Gerrard, Lewis. *Wah-to-Yah and the Taos Trail*. Introd. A.B. Guthrie, Jr. Norman: University of Oklahoma Press, 1971.

Gibson, Arrell Morgan. *The Santa Fe and Taos Colonies: Age of the Muses, 1900-1942*. Norman: University of Oklahoma Press, 1983.

————. *The West in the Life of the Nation*. Lexington, Massachusetts: D.C. Heath Co., 1976.

Gregg, Josiah. *Commerce of the Prairies*. Ed. Max L. Moorhead. Norman: University of Oklahoma Press, 1954.

Hammond George P. and Agapito Rey, Eds. *Narratives of the Coronado Expedition, 1540-1542*. Albuquerque: University of New Mexico Press, 1940.

Henderson, Alice Corbin. *The Penitentes*. New York: Harcourt, Brace, 1937.

James, Edwin. *Account of an Expedition from Pittsburgh to the Rocky Mountains, 1819-1820* in *Early Western Travels, 1748-1865*. Ed. Reuben G. Thwaites. Cleveland: Arthur H. Clark, Co., 1905.

Jeffers, Robinson. *Selected Poetry of Robinson Jeffers*. New York: Random House, 1938.

Jones, Billy M. *Health-Seekers in the Southwest, 1817-1900*. Norman: University of Oklahoma Press, 1967.

Kneese, Allen V. and F. Lee Brown. *The Southwest Under Stress: National Resource Development Issues in a Regional Setting*. Baltimore: Johns Hopkins Press, 1981.

Krutch, Joseph Wood. *The Desert Year*. Tucson: University of Arizona Press, 1985.

LaFarge, Oliver. *Laughing Boy*. Boston: Houghton Mifflin, 1929.

Lamar, Howard R. *The Far Southwest, 1846-1912*. New Haven: Yale University Press, 1966.

Lawrence, David H. *The Plumed Serpent*. London: W. Heinemann, 1955.

Long, Haniel. *Piñon Land*. New York: Duell, Sloan & Pearce, 1941.

Luhan, Mabel Dodge. *Winter in Taos*. New York: Harcourt, Brace & Co., 1935.

Lummis, Charles F. *Land of Poco Tiempo*. Albuquerque: University of New Mexico Press, 1952.

Meyer, Michael C. *Water in the Hispanic Southwest: A Social and Legal History, 1550-1850*. Tucson: University of Arizona Press, 1984.

Miller, Tom. *On the Border: Portraits of America's Southwestern Frontier.* Tucson: University of Arizona Press, 1985.

Ordóñez de Montalvo, Garci Rodríquez. "Las Sergas de Esplandían." Trans. Edward Everett Hale. *The Atlantic Monthly.* 82 (March, 1864), pp. 266-67.

Pike, Zebulon Montgomery. *The Expedition of Zebulon Montgomery Pike.* Ed. Elliott Coues. New York: Francis P. Harper, 1895, 2 vols.

Rea, Amadeo. *Once a River.* Tucson: University of Arizona Press, 1983.

Riggs, Lynn. *Green Grow the Lilacs.* New York: S. French, 1958.

Ruxton, George. *Life in the Far West.* Ed. LeRoy R. Hafen. Norman: University of Oklahoma Press, 1951.

Shaler, William. *Journal of a Voyage from China to the Northwestern Coast of America Made in 1804.* Claremont, California: Saunders Studio Press, 1935.

Waters, Frank. *The Colorado.* Athens, Ohio: Swallow Press, 1984.

Wiley, Peter and Robert Gottlieb. *Empires in the Sun: The Rise of the New American West.* Tucson: University of Arizona Press, 1985.

Woodin, Ann. *Home is the Desert.* Tucson: University of Arizona Press, 1984.

Janice Monk directs the Southwest Institute for Research on Women (SIROW) at the University of Arizona.

JANICE MONK & VERA NORWOOD

ANGLES OF VISION: ENHANCING OUR PERSPECTIVES ON THE SOUTHWEST

Geographers do not commonly venture into literary "terrain": we are concerned with more literal places and human responses to them. Over the last fifteen years, however, we have become increasingly interested in how the visions in people's minds shape what they see. In common with scholars in a number of other disciplines, we are beginning to recognize that environments and environmental responses assumed by earlier colleagues to represent universally shared values more often reflect only the perspective of the dominant culture—in the case of America, a culture limited to the values and perspectives of Anglo males. A multifocused perspective, considering how ethnicity, life stage, social class, and gender affect our angles of vision, is now enriching our field. Further, to learn how these factors have shaped perspectives on place in the past, we are turning to literature and the arts, including not only published works but also diaries, journals, memoirs, folk materials, and crafts. Such study offers alternative ways of looking at the world and develops a deeper understanding of human response to place.

This essay explores a particular angle of vision on a particular place: the perceptions of women writing about the Southwest over the last century. We draw on findings in our forthcoming book, a collaborative effort by a group of scholars representing geography, anthropology, art history and literary criticism, which investigates the

39

roles of gender and ethnicity in shaping women writers' and artists' responses to the region. We can present here only a brief summary, limited to the group's findings on women writers of the Southwest, but including cross-cultural comparisons of American Indian, Mexican-American and Anglo-American women.[1]

Although women and men do share some landscape visions, gender-focused study reveals distinct differences. Other essays in this book present descriptions of the nineteenth- and twentieth-century Southwest, primarily as it has been viewed by Anglo men (see Gibson particularly). Two common themes in their writing highlight the distinctiveness of women's work. First, men's tales of heroic adventures in a colorful landscape emphasize a place of fabulous qualities, but a place also improved by men's conquering escapades. Environmentalist writing constitutes a second theme among men who find value in the natural world of the desert, who celebrate solitude, isolation, and spareness. These writers are frequently concerned with preserving the region against encroaching civilization and tend to see the natural and human worlds in opposition to one another.

In these scenarios, women's writing appears as a very minor key, always paralleling the major outlines established by male voices. Further, only Anglo women are seen to have much to say about the region, particularly in the nineteenth and early twentieth centuries. Women, as well as men, however, have been stimulated to original creativity by the landscapes of the Southwest, producing works not always in keeping with the "central dogma" established by men. More importantly, although some landscape values have been shared among women of various class and ethnic backgrounds, differences can also be discerned as we compare women who come from the outside, women who have their heritage in the region, and those who have been culturally dispossessed in the past and are seeking today to regain a voice.

For contemporary American Indian writers, creative expression and the land are intimately linked: much of their inspiration, materials, themes, and processes of creation emanate directly from the land. For Chicana writers, possession of the land by their people and possession of a literary voice have been closely tied. Those few Hispanic women whose writings appeared in print before the 1960's, such as Cleofas Jaramillo or Fabiola Cabeza de Baca, mourn their loss of land, language, and culture, and hark back to an idealized pastoral Hispanic Southwest. Contemporary Chicana writers reclaim their cultural identity in part by claiming the urban landscape as their cultural space.

Among contemporary American Indian writers, Joy Harjo and Leslie
Silko both demonstrate this same capacity to draw on urban landscapes;
like their traditional forebears, they are able to find meaning in *all*
aspects of the landscape—not only the natural landscape but also
transcontinental highways, regional cities like Gallup, New Mexico, or,
as in this poem by Harjo, the Albuquerque airport:

> in the Albuquerque airport
> trying to find a flight
> to the old ariabi, third mesa
> TWA
>   is the only desk open
> bright lights outline new york,
>   chicago
> and the attendant doesn't know
> that the third mesa
> is a part of the center
> of the world
> and who are we
> just two indians
> at three in the morning
> trying to find a way back[2]

Although Harjo reveals the disjunctions between traditional landscapes
and the urban environments of the twentieth century Southwest, she
also argues that the problem of integration (of both people and place)
is not *her* people's, but that of the Anglo newcomers.

Anglo women who came to the Southwest in the first half of the
twentieth century found in the landscape inspiration, identity, and
energy that released their creativity. Mary Austin, for example, found
in the desert a psychic wholeness inspiring her best and most enduring
works, *The Land of Little Rain* and *The Land of Journeys' Ending*.
Willa Cather's introduction to the Southwest led to her acclaimed
regional novels whose distinctive structural forms, such as the
succession of pictures in *Death Comes for the Archbishop*, engrave
images of a specific landscape on the mind. Nancy Newhall, writer and
photographer, whose dedication to wilderness preservation emerged
after her introduction to the West by Ansel Adams, ultimately found in
the Southwest her *own*, more complex, vision of human connectedness
with the landscape. Newhall's Southwestern work emphasizes the
transitory nature of human settlement and the conflicting interests of
different groups of people, revealing concern for human conditions as
well as for land.[3]

By contrast with women from outside, the writing of many Anglo women with more binding ties to the Southwest than "enchantment" with exquisite vistas and exotic cultures is less celebratory of the inspirational qualities in the landscape. Writing about a constantly changing region, Margaret Collier Graham, Frances Gillmor, and Joan Didion are more concerned with accepting a demanding and difficult landscape on its own terms and creating arts based on survival within limitations established by the environment. Didion's work, *Play It As It Lays*, exemplifies this type in its portrayals of both modern Los Angeles landscapes and Nevada desert landscapes of her heroine's adult trials and childhood memories.[4]

Although the landscape has served in different ways to liberate women's creativity, their responses reveal common bases for this liberation which we can only sketch here. One recurring metaphor is a vision of the natural world as a woman. Unlike the dominant male meanings given to the same metaphor, this woman is neither a virgin to be raped or tamed nor a fruitful mother; rather, she embodies traits that give the women a sense of their own complexity, power, and worth. Mary Austin, for example, portrays the desert as a strong woman who has not been and cannot be mastered—in such a portrayal the vast and undominated scale of the land liberates woman from strictures of traditional femininity silencing her voice. Nor is the land/woman confined to a narrow range of roles. For Alice Corbin Henderson, the land can be an old woman, ancient and peaceful, "blinking and blind in the sun . . . who mumbles her beads/ and crumbles to stone." Contemporary Chicana poet Pat Mora finds all these meanings and more in the female deserts that serve as teachers, healers, or *curanderas*, the wise women who mediate between human beings and nature and bring the gift of power and magic to the writer.[5]

Association of landscape and gender extends to the built environment. For Carmen Tafolla and Rina Garcia Rocha, for example, the city is a woman. These writers recognize that men *and* women in both their culture and Anglo culture often describe cities as female, but they distinguish between the stereotype of indolence often applied to border towns in particular and their own more complex vision of a woman/city which may be ragged, indifferent, or wicked, but also toils long hours at menial tasks. Although such city images provoke ambivalence in Chicanas, they also enable them to express their own search for identity and struggle with oppression. For women, then, identification with a complex female landscape frees them from narrow conventions, and releases their creative voices.[6]

A second aspect of landscape fostering women's creativity is the erotically charged energy they see emanating from the land, an energy most forcefully and consistently infusing the writing of American Indian women. For them the land is sensual and sensate, the embodiment of spirits actively communicating with people and experiencing the critical events of their lives. Sexual encounters with the land serve both to release and channel creative wildness within. Anglos and Chicanas, however, also find freedom from sexual constraints in the landscape. Pat Mora vividly images their response:

> The desert is no lady.
> She screams at the spring sky,
> dances with her skirts high,
> kicks sand, flings tumbleweeds,
> digs her nails into all flesh.
> Her unveiled lust fascinates the sun.[7]

The above is only a brief sketch of the dynamic relationship between women's creativity and their landscape experiences. Our findings also consider the specific landscapes or aspects of landscape women writers value. Cross-cultural comparisons are intriguing, but also problematic. Many Anglos bring to the region Euro-American traditions: they look at American Indian architecture, for example, and see esthetically pleasing structures that invite manipulations of volume and shape, light and shadow. For Indians, the same buildings may be read as a network of social relationships. Anglos in general make more of the light and space in the region than either American Indians or Chicanas. One must be careful, however, of making simple distinctions between the Anglos and other ethnic groups. For although outsider Anglo women were instrumental in formulating a tradition of the Southwest landscape as exotic and awe-inspiring, a tradition they shared with men, Anglos who lived in the region developed landscape attitudes similar to the longer-dwelling Chicanas and Indians. Thus, outsider Mary Austin celebrates the virtues of a sandstorm, but insider Mary Kidder Rak expresses practical concerns about the next rain, echoing the visions of Indians and Chicanas.[8]

Although they may have brought images of a lush garden down the Santa Fe Trail, Anglo women settlers rather quickly gave up such paradisiacal visions, feeling they could not count on the land as a traditional, reliable agricultural home. They came to respond to scarcity and admire women's adaptations to the problematic landscape of droughts, Santa Ana winds, and crop failures. By contrast, for the

Chicanas, the garden was, and continues to be, located in the Southwest. Thus, just as Anglos and American Indians look at the same landscape and locate different values in what they see, so too Chicanos and Anglos do not always mean the same type of place when they refer to a "garden." In the case of the writers we studied, Chicanas' longer tenancy on the land and greater familiarity with indigenous plants helps them locate gardens where Anglos see only arid plains. Such findings reveal the importance of considering context in any generalization about what kind of landscape "women" value, and the need for more scholarship beyond a focus defined in Anglo-generated terms of reference and generalizations based on initial responses of outsiders.

As noted above, environmentalist values are strongly voiced in male writers' work on the Southwest. A number of the Anglo women writers (for example, Mary Austin, Mabel Dodge Luhan, Nancy Newhall, and Frances Gillmor) also criticize modern development in the Southwest. The environmental movement has been questioned for its Anglo middle-class emphasis and for its focus on the preservation of wilderness for an elite population; such a bias does appear in the responses of some of the Anglo women we have examined. Nevertheless, the women are not monolithic in their views, and a number go beyond the limitations of environmentalist philosophy in their descriptions and reproductions of valued landscapes. Rather than engaging in attempts to "edit" people out of the natural environments of the region, to preserve a trackless wilderness as a stage for heroic challenges, women often envision landscapes that speak to appropriate human tenancy on the land, valuing built environments in keeping with the requirements of the place and respectful of natural limitations. Thus, although Nancy Newhall initially shared with Ansel Adams an appreciation for grand heroic vistas, once she became familiar with the lifestyles of people in the Southwest she was much more concerned with creating images of appropriate human responses. So while Adams worked to eliminate people from his photographs of Tucson's Mission San Xavier del Bac, Newhall was interested in the ways people inhabit the church.

Such concern for the importance of vernacular landscapes is shared by women of the three cultural groups we studied. Patricia Preciado Martin's *Images and Conversations* reveals strong values among Chicanas for a landscape that appropriately balances organic environments with human dwellings:

In 1858 José M. Sosa built a small residence for his family on Main Street—Tucson's old Camino Real. . . . In 1878 the property was sold to Leopoldo Carrillo . . . in time he dug a well, built corrals and chicken houses, planted herbs and flowers—and a fig tree. The fig tree, nourished by the sweet water drawn from the well, flourished in that desert garden. Through the years it grew, its spreading branches finally embracing the garden walls. On warm summer nights, the family would gather outdoors to enjoy the cool evening breeze. Undisturbed by the noise or concerns of modern urbanites, they would count the stars and fall asleep beneath the protective canopy of the sky and the fig tree.

Through the years the fig tree continued to grow and give fruit to succeeding generations. In the twentieth century a bustling Mexican neighborhood grew up around the house of the fig tree. It was a community of vitality and culture and tradition, built with the love and labor of those who dwelled there. But the laughter and songs of the descendants of those early Mexican pioneers would in time be silenced by the bulldozers of progress and urban renewal. Only the Sosa-Carillo house would be spared, standing alone in a wilderness of asphalt, brick, and glass—mute evidence of the past. And miraculously that same fig tree still branched and flowered in stubborn affirmation of those families who gave it root, greening forth in solitude—a symbol of history and nostalgia in a modern wasteland of concrete, an inheritance which still gives sustenance to those of us who pass this way.[9]

American Indian writers like Luci Tapahonso likewise value the everyday places they experience, in which the forces of nature and human lives are organically intertwined. So, in "A Breeze Swept Through," a poem about the birth of her daughter, a breeze, embodying the woman of dawn, sweeps through the kitchen in celebration of the child. Thus across cultures in the Southwest we find women endorsing the ways that various landscapes speak to and for ordinary people and daily life.[10]

In stressing the importance vernacular landscapes play in women's writing, we do not imply that American Indians and Chicanas do not locate value in pristine, untenanted nature, nor that Anglo women's valuation of such a landscape has been limited to adoption of dominant male attitudes. As a group, the women we studied feel quite comfortable in and value highly the untenanted natural world. In this way, they contradict standard images of women, particularly of Anglos, as fearful in the presence of the wild. These women do not conform to stereotypes that would restrict their movement beyond the confines of local habitation. In fact, among the writers, there is a strong tradition in all three cultures of actively seeking experience in landscapes perceived to be less safe for women; although urban environments offer one such set, wilderness seems to be more consistently mentioned as the place for adventure.

Nevertheless, though all the women seek adventures of sexual liberation, cultural differences are evident in the goals of such liberation. For the American Indian writer, wilderness presents a place in which to learn how to accept her own sexuality and control it within acceptable bounds. For the Chicana, the wild landscape, particularly the desert, seems to be a place to escape and defy socially restrictive gender roles, but she is not often able to bring this wilderness back incorporated into her social life. For the Anglo woman, the wilderness seems to offer a place to retreat from social prescriptions about gender roles, rather than to defy them, and to provide a sanctuary and momentary space for erotic freedom. Perhaps because the cultural proscriptions against liberating female sexuality remain so strong, and because many Anglo writers have not returned to their own versions of nature goddesses, such as the American Indians have in the Changing Woman figure or the Chicanas have in the *curandera,* they are not yet able to speak as freely about the values of wilderness to women as their counterparts in the Southwest.

Women then, as well as men, seek personal transformation through interaction with the landscape. Unlike the classic male visions of the Southwest, however, their searches are not cast in terms of heroic dominance or of a retreat from human life into solitude within the deserts. Rather, they celebrate the vernacular, see the landscape as a context for human life, and seek to adapt to natural exigencies. They maintain a sense of personal vulnerability to and reciprocity with the landscape. Nancy Newhall's celebration of the transforming powers of the desert, based on absorption into the land, perhaps best expresses women's "angle of vision" on the Southwest:

Noon in the desert is a vast blaze overhead and a hard glow below. You are shut in by vast distances of light. You walk in the focus of the sun's rays. You are clothed in sun; sun glows in your blood, until even your bones feel incandescent. . . . You feel in your body why the desert wears grey, and why it blooms with such vital brilliance.[11]

ENDNOTES

[1]This essay is based on the editors' introduction and conclusion to Vera Norwood and Janice Monk (eds.), *The Desert is No Lady: Women's Visions of Southwestern*

Landscapes, 1880-1980 (New Haven: Yale University Press, 1987).

[2]Joy Harjo, "3 AM" in *Southwest: A Contemporary Anthology*, ed. Karl and Jane Kopp (Albuquerque: Red Earth Press, 1977), p. 173.

[3]Mary Austin, *The Land of Little Rain* (Albuquerque: University of New Mexico Press, 1974) and *The Land of Journeys' Ending* (Tucson: University of Arizona Press, 1983) cited in Lois Rudnick, "Re-Mything the Land: Anglo Expatriate Women in the Southwest," in Norwood and Monk (eds.); Willa Cather, *Death Comes for the Archbishop* (New York: Knopf, 1927) cited in Judith Fryer, "Desert, Rock, Shelter, Legend: Willa Cather's Novels of the Southwest," in Norwood and Monk (eds.).

[4]Joan Didion, *Play It As It Lays* (New York: Bantam, 1971) cited in Vera Norwood, "Crazy Quilt Lives: Frontier Sources for Southwestern Women's Literature," in Norwood and Monk (eds.).

[5]Alice Corbin Henderson, Untitled, *Red Earth: Poems of New Mexico* (Chicago: Ralph Seymour, 1920), cited in Rudnick; Pat Mora, *Chants* (Houston: Arte Público Press, 1984) cited in Diana Rebolledo, "Tradition and Mythology: Signatures of Landscape in Chicana Literature," in Norwood and Monk (eds.).

[6]Carmen Tafolla, "Get Your Tortillas Together" (no pub., 1976) and Rina Garcia Rocha, *Hojas Poeticas* (Tucson: Scorpion Press, 1977) cited in Rebolledo.

[7]Pat Mora, "Unrefined," *Chants* (Houston: Arte Público Press, 1984), cited in Rebolledo.

[8]Mary Kidder Rak, *A Cowman's Wife* (New York: Houghton Mifflin, 1934), cited in Norwood.

[9]Patricia Preciado Martin, *Images and Conversations: Mexican Americans Recall a Southwestern Past* (Tucson: University of Arizona Press, 1983), pp. 9-10, cited in Rebolledo.

[10]Luci Tapahonso, "A Breeze Swept Through," *A Sense of Myself* (unpublished master's thesis, University of New Mexico, 1983) cited in Patricia Clark Smith, "Earthy Relations, Carnal Knowledge: Southwestern American Indian Women Writers and Landscape," in Norwood and Monk (eds.).

[11]Nancy Newhall, "Organ Pipe Cactus National Monument," *Arizona Highways*, 30, no. 1 (January 1954), pp. 14-16 cited in MaLin Wilson, "Walking on the Desert in the Sky: Nancy Newhall's Words and Images," in Norwood and Monk (eds.).

Tey Diana Rebolledo directs the Women Studies Program at the University of New Mexico, where she is also Associate Professor of Spanish.

TEY DIANA REBOLLEDO

HISPANIC WOMEN WRITERS OF THE SOUTHWEST: TRADITION AND INNOVATION

nd its settlement, women are
d mothers or cultural workers.
ve pioneers, madonnas of the
the saloons. Hispanic women
Western mythology are often
chili queen" from across the
works silently at her task.
nish cultural tradition existed
to take up the land, and clearly
n all the roles of pioneers,
a period of some four hundred

ving in the Southwest are the
dition, of personal and historic
ons of Hispanic women before
nections between contemporary
Hispanic women writing before
c as well as contextual material
is discussion will also point out
e two groups. Hispanic women
ivided into two generations: the
en writing before 1950, and the

second of writers who come to the forefront after the Chicano Renaissance of the late 1960's.[1]

There is little information at present about early Hispanic women writers, but in the 1930's through the 1950's several books were published by New Mexican women writers dealing with local customs, foods, history and folklore. These books are first-person accounts incorporating stories and tales of older relatives and acquaintances, thus extending the "personal narrative" further into the past. This "first" generation of writers consists of a very small group of women who were Hispanic, generally well-educated, who came from upper-class, often landed families, and wrote in English. They were influenced by the work being done collecting folklore and folklife in the 1930's, particularly by the Federal Writers Project. Cleofas Jaramillo, Nina Otero Warren, and Fabiola Cabeza de Baca are three women considered here because their work shares similar characteristics and because in some senses they share a common perspective. All three women have a romanticized attitude towards the rural landscape. All share a sense of the passing away of their Hispanic culture and their language. They mention little about the women in their families, although what they do communicate to us gives us a rare glimpse into the women's lives of the time. They have a definitely ethnocentric view of the Indian roots of their culture, clearly defining themselves as Spanish and looking upon the Indian as being both inferior and apart from themselves. Their sense of consciousness of social issues is not clear. They are enclosed and socialized by a process where women are expected to perform in traditional ways, yet none of the three actually did.

Of the three writers, Nina Otero Warren is perhaps the most romantic. She concentrated on quaint folkloric vignettes praising the disappearing Spanish heritage. Her book *Old Spain in Our Southwest* (1936) evokes days of gay caballeros, fiestas, and señoritas. Yet she also feels change and loss: "This Southwestern country, explored and settled nearly four hundred years ago by a people who loved nature, worshipped God and feared no evil, is still a region of struggles."[2] Her narrative is also highly sentimental and most things of value are presented as end products of Spain, not of Mexico, and certainly not of the Indian heritage.

Cabeza de Baca's *We Fed Them Cactus* (1949) reveals a concern with the economic and social fortunes of Hispanic New Mexicans living through the change from Hispanic New Mexico to Anglo New Mexico.[3] The book's title itself is symbolic since the cactus appears as a central symbol not only for Cabeza de Baca, but also for many of the contemporary women writers. The book refers, on one level, to the drought of 1918 when Hispanic farmers fed cactus to their cattle for survival. On another level, it refers to the Hispanos themselves as survivors able to weather misfortunes. The book is a historical account of the acquisition of the land in New Mexico, the change of control in 1848 when New Mexico became part of the United States, the arrival of homesteaders, the destruction of the land due to inadequate land practices, and finally the loss of the land by the Hispanos: a loss linked to the loss of a traditional way of life. At the beginning of the narrative, the New Mexico landscape is a rich, nourishing, fruitful Garden of Eden, a varied topography with mountains, desert, wooded lands and sweet water springs gushing from inside the earth, even though rain is scarce:

From Canon del Agua Hill to Luciano Mesa, the vegetation includes juniper, piñon, yucca, mesquite, sagebrush, grama and buffalo grasses as well as lemita, prickly pear and pitahaya. There are wild flowers in abundance, and when the spring comes rainy, the earth abounds in all colors imaginable. The fields of oregano and cactus, when in full bloom, can compete with the loveliest of gardens [page 2].

Throughout Cabeza de Baca's narrative, it is clear that her family depends upon the land and that the relationship to land and weather is dominant:

Money in our lives was not important; rain was important . . . rain for us made history. It brought to our minds days of plenty, of happiness and security, and in recalling past events, if they fell on rainy years, we never failed to stress that fact. The droughts were as impressed on our souls as the rains. When we spoke of the Armistice of World War I, we always said, 'The drought of 1918 when the Armistice was signed [pages 14-15].'

She also describes what is left of her vanishing people as she traces the loss of the Spanish land grants. Bitterness over lost land and nostalgia over lost culture are implicit in her description of the desert wasteland compared to what before she saw as paradise:

The land, between the years 1932-1935, became a dust bowl. The droughts, erosion of the land, the unprotected soil and overgrazing of pastures had no power over the winds . . . . There was not a day of respite from the wind . . . . In the mornings upon rising from bed, one's body was imprinted on the sheets which were covered with sand . . . . The whole world around us was a thick cloud of dust. The sun was invisible and one would scarcely venture into the outdoors for fear of breathing the foul grit. The winds blew all day and they blew all night, until every plant which had survived was covered by hills of sand [page 177].

Thus *We Fed Them Cactus* is an extraordinary account of the evolution and change suffered by a people, expressed through landscape.

One of the strong women who emerges from another narrative of Cabeza de Baca's, *The Good Life,* is a person she calls the Herb Woman. Active in both Hispanic and Indian communal lives, she was a woman of knowledge and wisdom of the natural world. In Hispanic folklore the *curandera* (medicine woman, herb woman, healer) is a woman who has always been more free to come and go. And although many curanderas did not know how to write, they stored their knowledge in their incredible memories. Cabeza de Baca writes:

The medicine woman seemed so old and wrinkled to Doña Paula and she wondered how old she was. No one remembered when she was born. She had been a slave in the García family for two generations and that was all anyone knew. She had not wanted her freedom, and yet she had always been free. She had never married but she had several sons and daughters.[4]

This curandera is the keeper of secrets and the preserver of delicate ecological balances. When asked about some herbs she carries with her, she answers: "These are getting so scarce that I only brought you a few leaves: the men pull them up as weeds."[5]

The curandera has been an important social and cultural force in Hispanic tradition since the colonial period and continues to play a strong role in daily life as well as in folklore and myth. We will see later how this figure has been revived by the contemporary writers.

Cleofas Jaramillo in her books *Shadows of the Past* (1941) and *Romance of a Little Village Girl* (1955) states similar concerns to those of Otero Warren and Cabeza de Baca. Her writing, she says, was stimulated by the artistic climate of Santa Fe in the early 1940's. She explains, "Writing and art are contagious in this old town. We have caught the fever from our famous 'cinco pintores' and author Mary Austin, and some of us have the courage to try. It is only by trying that we learn what we can do."[6] Interesting too is that as an author she is writing in English, as do the other two, and at the beginning of her story she expresses her feeling of foreigness in language which echoes the outcome of her autogiography—from rootedness in the land to alienation in the city.

What is most definite about these writers is their clear sense of the passing of the Spanish culture, and their need to record and clarify it before it is totally lost. And often this sense of loss is reflected in the landscape. Fabiola Cabeza de Baca writes in *We Fed Them Cactus*:

The Hispano has almost vanished from the land . . . but the names of hills, rivers, arroyos, canyons and defunct plazas linger as monuments to a people who pioneered into the land of the buffalo and the Comanche. These names have undergone many changes but are still known and repeated. Very likely many of those who pronounce them daily are unaware that they are of Spanish origin [page 66].

After these books were published in the '30's, '40's, and early '50's, the Hispanic women writers of the Southwest lapsed into a Sleeping Beauty silence. It was not until after the Chicano Civil Rights Movement and the accompanying literary renaissance of the late 1960's that Hispanic (now Chicana) women writers once again found their voices. In the intervening time many things had changed. A recognition of the value of the intermixture of races, a pride in the Indian as well as the Spanish past, a desire to retain culture in the form of language, a recognition of the richness of bilingualism and biculturalism, a pride in the legacy of history left to the Mexican American resulted in a literary outpouring in many directions. Women writing after 1968 wrote of social and political issues and struggled with who they were. They took as role models revolutionary heroines such as La Adelita. They resuscitated Nahuatl goddesses who represented power and authority, they found old myths, created new ones and reinterpreted the ones they didn't like, such as that of La Malinche.[7] The female tradition and women-to-women relationships, particularly among family members, became accentuated. And the writers continued to explore their relationship to the landscape and the land. However, they no longer solely explored rural landscapes, but also the urban ones.

As Chicanos lost political and economic power, they also lost social stability. Our neighborhoods in the city declined until today the word *barrio* (or neighborhood) to some signifies a slum. In the West the continuous waves of new immigrant populations from Mexico often swelled these Spanish-speaking neighborhoods. These immigrants maintained the connections with Mexico and reinforced bonds of language and culture, but at the same time they pushed social and economic possibilities and services beyond their means. In many barrios life became even more of a struggle. Often the Chicanos felt themselves to be (and were) a people who had become a minority in a land they once considered theirs, rejected because of language and race, exploited and unrepresented in the midst of the myth of democracy. This is part of the urban scene that the Chicana writer sees and reflects. Angela de Hoyos explores this in her poem "La gran ciudad," as she details the struggle of a single mother who has arrived in the city looking for opportunity, only to find racial prejudice cutting into her survival. She reiterates the stereotyping of the language barrier in an ironic comment on the democratic ideal.

> No one told me.
> So how was I to know
> that in the paradise
> of crisp white cities
> snakes still walk
> upright?
> . . . .
> when I couldn't pay the rent
> the landlord came to see me.
> . . . .
> Ain't you Meskin?
> How come you speak such good English?
> Y yo le contesto
> Because I'm, Spanglo, that's why.
> . . . .
> So where is the paradise?
> In the land of the mighty
> where is the shining
> -The EQUAL-opportunity?[8]

These Chicana writers, as did the earliest Hispanic writers, express mixed emotions about their environment: both a sense of alienation and one of fond memories. The early writers tended to look to the past when life was more secure and stable. Present-day writers see current reality without great nostalgia. Beverly Silva's poem, "The Roaches Came from Everywhere," chronicles an urban struggle with some sense of humor and ultimate survival.

> over
> above
> behind
> between
> around
> below

it was a lesson in prepositions to ponder them.
Big ones
small ones
medium sized ones
families & communities of them invaded our apartment.
. . . .
At night they crawled from all the cracks
to cover our walls like some grotesque canvas
painted by a madman.

To move wasn't possible
we had to fight.
. . . .
The roaches became my nemesis.
Sharing these vermin bound me forever to my neighbors.
The temporariness of our situations became enhanced
by rejections of our mutual suffering,
pretense of waiting lists for better apartments,
or savings for deposit money.
Easier to live with roaches when:

We're going to move from here any time now.[9]

On the other hand, this poem by Evangelina Vigil shows that the barrio can also hold fond memories.

in the San Juan Projects
they spray-painted all the buildings
pastel pink, blue, green, pale yellow, gray
. . . .
no sooner than had the building wall/canvasses been painted clean
did barrio kids take to carving new inspirations
and chuco hieroglyphics and new figure drawings of naked women
        and their parts
and messages for all
"la Diana es puta"
"el Lalo es joto"
y que "la Chelo se deja"
decorated by hearts and crosses
and war communication
among rivaling gangs
. . . .
pretty soon kids took to just plain peeling plastic pastel paint
to unveil historical murals
of immediate past well-remembered:
más monas encueradas

and "Lupe loves Tony"
"always and forever"
"Con Safos"
y "sin Safos"
y que "El Chuy es relaje"
. . . .
secret fear in every child
que "su nombre apareciera allí"
[that her or his name would appear there][10]

This writing of names in Pachuco hieroglyphics on urban buildings is a way of putting a stamp of identity on the landscape. The link with old traditions and a sense of survival in landscape can also be seen in a short story by Patricia Preciado Martin, "The Journey." The story is structured on the glaring contrast between old Tucson and new Tucson, the disappearance of the old barrio standing as the central metaphor. The elderly aunt "Tía" lives in the "Martin Luther King Jr. Apartments, Low Cost Housing for the Elderly," an ironic comment on the success of the Black Civil Rights Movement and the relative lack of advancement for Chicanos, since almost all those who live there are Hispanic *viejitos*. The young Chicana in the story takes her aunt shopping and the route is always the same: past the landmarks of old Hispanic Tucson. Each building, each house is peopled by memories of those who lived their lives there. Each is also sharply connected to an ironic voice of today.

On Ochoa Street we turn west again and walk toward the gleaming white towers of the Cathedral. San Augustín. The Dove of the Desert. The pigeons flutter over our heads when the noon bells chime. Sr. Enríquez, the old bell chimer, died long ago. He climbed the rickety stairs to the bell towers three times a day for more years than anyone could remember. One day he climbed up and played the Noon Angelus and never climbed down again. They found him with the bell rope still in his hands. Now the angelus is a recorded announcement.[11]

The freeway which cuts through the center of the Spanish-speaking barrio is a symbol of the destruction wrought by modern civilization, and particularly of those planners who looked upon the barrios as slums and appropriate places to build freeways or as fit places for urban renewal. Preciado Martin says: "The freeway has cut the river from the people. The freeway blocks the sunshine. The drone of the traffic buzzes like a giant unsleeping bee. A new music in the barrio [page 5]."

The aunt's journey always leads to the same place:

the house where she was born. The pace of Tía quickens now. I follow her, carrying the straw bag laden with groceries. We walk past the Concert Hall to the vast parking lot of the Community Center Complex. A billboard reads: CONCERT TONIGHT. ALICE COOPER. SOLD OUT. We stop in the middle of the parking lot. The winter sun is warm. The heat rises from the black asphalt. The roar of the freeway is even more distinct. It is the end of the journey. I know what Tía will say.

'Aquí estaba mi casita. It was my father's house. And his father's house before that. They built it with their own hands with adobes made from the mud of the river. All their children were born here. I was born here. It was a good house, a strong house. When it rained, the adobes smelled like the good clean earth. . . . See here! I had a fig tree growing. In the summer I gave figs to the neighbors and the birds. . . . I had a bougainvilla: it was so beautiful! Brilliant red. And I had roses and a little garden. Right here where I am standing my comadres and I would sit and visit in the evenings.'

As they turn to go, the niece (who has become the recipient of the cultural heritage) for the first time sees something new.

'Tía. Tía.' I call. 'Ven.' She turns and comes toward me.
'Look!' I say excitedly. 'There is a flower that has pushed its way through the asphalt! It is blooming!'
'Ah, mihijita,' she says at last. Her eyes are shining.
'You have found out the secret of our journeys.'
'What secret, Tía?'
'Que las flores siempre ganan. The flowers always win [page 6].'

The sense of hope, of regeneration exemplified by the flower breaking through the asphalt, can be seen in the second response of contemporary Chicana writers as they return to integration with the land and with nature as seen in their portrayal of the landscape.

The new generation of writers, in particular poet Pat Mora, use the link with nature and with the desert landscape as a way of defining selfhood. They use their perceptions of the landscape, particularly the desert, and the figure of the curandera as mediator between nature and people. In addition, the relationship between sexuality and the land, missing before in the earlier writers, is explicitly detailed, as in this poem by Mora:

> The desert is no lady
> She screams at the spring sky,
> dances with her skirts high,
> kicks sand, flings tumbleweed,
> digs her nails into all flesh.
> Her unveiled lust fascinates the sun.[12]

It is in Mora's poetry that both tradition and innovation reach their most complete expression. Her landscape is always portrayed in female terms and there is generally a human present: often a wise woman with knowledge to impart. "Curandera" is a text which shows the connection between the land, the mediator who gathers wild plants for healing use and the magical powers this woman has. Here the new generation picks up the myths and folklore of the early writers, but they are changed and transformed. The *curandera* gathers and imparts nature's secrets, she represents both intuition and rational knowledge. Within her rests especially the knowledge of the female tradition. She is also in harmony with both order and disorder. If witches can be a force for total chaos and are closely associated with wild manifestations such as storms and untamed animals, then the curandera is a witch and she is not a witch. That is, she has the power to control those forces, but she chooses to heal. Thus she is both the center and on the edge. In Mora's poem the *curandera* is associated with the owl, but also with the coyote. She eats chopped cactus and brushes the sand from her bed, both reminiscent of the symbolic meanings of the cactus and the import of the sand storm in Cabeza de Baca's narrative.

> They think she lives alone
> on the edge of town in a two-room house
> where she moved when her husband died
> at thirty-five of a gunshot wound
> in the bed of another woman. The curandera
> and house have aged together to the rhythm
> of the desert.
> . . . .
> Like a large black bird, she feeds on
> the desert, gathering herbs for her basket.
> Her days are slow, days of grinding
> dried snake into powder,

of crushing wild bees to mix with white wine.
And the townspeople come, hoping
to be touched by her ointments,
her hands, her prayers, her eye.
She listens to their stories, and she listens
to the desert, always, to the desert.
. . . .
At night she cooks chopped cactus
and brews more tea. She brushes a layer
of sand from her bed, sand which covers
the table, stove, floor. She blows
the statues clean, the candles out.
Before sleeping, she listens to the message
of the owl and the coyote. She closes her eyes
and breathes with the mice and snakes
and wind.[13]

The *curandera* is not merely a figure of the past for contemporary Chicanos because today curanderas still thrive. Yet she is in some senses the repository of past learning, past history. Mora plays upon nostalgia for the archetypal, integrated world and on the nourishment and enrichment that magic, tradition, and fantasy offer. The magic passes from the curandera to the poet. It is the poet who will then pass on that knowledge to the reader, through the act of writing.

Thus for contemporary writers the relationship to their environment and their cultural tradition in these writings shows a nexus with their past as well as introduction of change. The early writers saw the desert as a powerful element, but also as a bountiful garden with wild plants to be harvested and used either as nourishment or for healing. The mediator and gatherer of this power was woman. The contemporary writer follows this tradition, incorporating a new consciousness of heritage, an acknowledgement of the importance of the Indian past. The sense of female tradition and female connectedness is also of prime importance since that indefinable heritage too often lost in history books must be recollected, organized and captured in words. In both generations there is a realization that finally the rich oral tradition held by so many Hispanic/Chicana women must be put into writing.

Chicana literature is an optimistic one. The power to make changes comes from the ability to speak out and these women are finding their voices. Rooted or rootless, they are surviving in ways that are creative and strong. Their voices, lost to them for many years, form a strong collective discourse. They are the realization of their traditions and the innovators of a new, more open discourse. The image of the cactus, enduring, stong with inner reserves and resources, is a recurring one in Chicana literature. It is the Chicana herself as well as her culture. Beverly Silva's urban poem "The Cactus" connects the natural world and the urban world, the early writers and the contemporary ones. In the Southwest the cactus survives, grows, fruits and nourishes: this is precisely what these writers are doing in their literature.

November sunshine floods my kitchen window.
    The plants thrive.
    The lemon tree bursts with ripe fruit.
    i measure the cactus.
    Five inches of new growth
    since that cold January afternoon
    i found it.
    Lone spindly thing like all the life here
    on Second St.
    uprooted and cast off in a corner of the alley
    between Taconazo and my apartments.
    i brought it home
    laid wet paper towels on its roots
    not knowing then
    that almost nothing can kill a cactus.
    i planted this dried up spike in a plastic pot
    with dirt from the parking lot of this next door dance hall.
    Taconazo dirt.
    The cactus grows.
    i eat nopalitos every morning with my breakfast.[14]

ENDNOTES

[1]Parts of this paper are from a longer essay that will appear in *The Desert is No Lady*, Janice Monk and Vera Norwood, eds., (New Haven: Yale University Press [in press, 1987]).

The terms Hispanic, Chicana, Mexican American mean different things both historically and ideologically. All refer to people of Spanish descent: Mexican American refers specifically to those of Mexican ancestry who either came from Mexico to live in the United States or who are descended from Mexican parents or grandparents. Hispanic is a more generic term used to denote Spanish speaking or descended people. Chicano is a relatively new term in general use since the 1960's. It is another term for Mexican American but it carries with it an ideological sense of pride of all heritages (Spanish, Indian, Mexican and born in the United States) and a pride in Spanish and Indian cultures and languages. In this paper I have tried to use the terms historically or as the writers called themselves. Chicano is a generic term encompassing both females and males, while Chicana refers only to women.

The Chicano Renaissance resulted in an outpouring of writing and publishing, mostly by male writers. Except for a few well-known writers, the women were mostly published in journals devoted to Chicano literature or they self-published. Many early anthologies of American women writers usually include no Chicana writers. The effect of the lack of publishing and distribution is that while some Chicana writers are fairly well-known in the West/Southwest, most write in relative obscurity. In the last few years, however, writing and publishing by and about Chicana writers has virtually exploded and the creative material grows daily.

[2]Nina Otero Warren, *Old Spain in Our Southwest* (New York: Harcourt Brace and Co., 1936), p. 3.

[3]Fabiola Cabeza de Baca, *We Fed Them Cactus* (1954; rpt., Albuquerque: The University of New Mexico Press, 1979), p. 66. Subsequent page references are to the 1979 edition.

[4]Fabiola Cabeza de Baca, *The Good Life* (Santa Fe: The Museum of New Mexico Press, 1949), p. 14.

[5]Cabeza de Baca, p. 17.

[6]Cleofas Jaramillo, *Romance of a Little Village Girl* (San Antonio: Naylor Co., 1955), p. 167.

[7]La Adelita is a Mexican revolutionary heroine commemorated in song and poetry. La Malinche is the Indian woman who translated for Hernán Cortes during the conquest of Mexico.

[8]Angela de Hoyos, *Chicano Poems for the Barrio* (San Antonio: M and A Editions, 1975), pp. 12-13.

[9]Beverly Silva, *The Second St. Poems* (Ypsilanti, MI: Bilingual Press, 1983), pp. 38-39.

[10]Evangelina Vigil, *Thirty 'n Seen a Lot* (Houston: Arte Público Press, 1982), pp. 62-63. Bracketed comment is author's.

[11]Patricia Preciado Martin, "The Journey," *La Confluencia* 3, No. 3-4 (1980), 4. Further references are in the text.

[12]Pat Mora, *Chants* (Houston: Arte Público Press, 1984), p. 8.

[13]Mora, p. 26.

[14]Silva, p. 77.

David Lavender, who spent his early years working in the mines and ranches around Telluride, Colorado, has written twenty-five books about the West.

DAVID LAVENDER

THE TYRANNY OF FACTS

I would like to start this discussion of legitimate and illegitimate historical fiction writing with an anecdote about Hollywood. The year—I was told all this by one of the participants—was 1954, the sesquicentennial of Lewis and Clark's crossing of the continent one hundred and fifty years earlier. What a Western epic! Two movie companies, each initially unaware of the other's intentions, decided to exploit the feat. Both had made a considerable investment before a hideous historical truth dawned. During Lewis and Clark's remarkable crossing there had been no in-fighting among the personnel, no love problems with nubile red maidens. No enemies of their country had tried to stir up the wild tribes of the wilderness into stopping them. They just went to the Pacific and came back again. Now, what kind of story was that?

By this time the race between the companies to reach the market first was common knowledge, and neither wished to lose face by backing down. Hoping to jazz up their films, both secretly hired new script writers, new producers, new directors. One of them also hired, as a consultant, the able and popular historian Harold Lamb. The fact that Lamb's specialty was the Orient and not the American West was evidently not considered relevant. When a spy from the rival group discovered who he was, he was overjoyed. "They've hired a historian," he chortled to his colleagues. "He'll screw things up for sure!"

What the spy was saying, of course, was that Harold Lamb, a conscientious historian, would not flirt with drama by bending the facts of the Lewis and Clark exploration—those hard, ineluctable, tyrannical facts of record—out of their true shape.

This tension arises every time a fiction writer turns to history for inspiration. How is he or she going to handle verifiable reality?

There are various ways of avoiding the dilemma. The easiest is to rely heavily on costuming. Achieve verisimilitude by piling up mountains of carefully chosen local color details and then let the characters carry on as the plot requires in this semi-authentic, but not specifically historic setting. Such a device is marvelously employed in parts of Larry McMurtry's recent, many-paged, best-selling *Lonesome Dove*.

Another device, used by such disparate writers as Gore Vidal and Irving Stone, is to choose a protagonist so well known that no writer in his right mind would dare be either accidentally mistaken or deliberately untruthful. Let's take Irving Stone as an example. After thoroughly immersing himself in his subject, Stone picks out a clearly defined line to follow through life's normal, messy clutter. He downplays inconvenient facts. He plays up those that fit his narrative. The only things he invents are dialogue, inner monologues, and such minor incidents as might occur in anyone's daily existence. When academic critics raise objections to what they call his maneuverings, Stone retorts imperturbably (if he bothers to retort at all) by asking them to point out one major concrete error. Perhaps he can't document conversation and thoughts. Still, he says, he has been faithful to the spirit of things, and his work should be accepted in that light.

It is just possible he is correct. I recall being in Rome, in the Sistine Chapel, a year or so after the publication of his novel about Michelangelo, *The Agony and the Ecstasy*. The place was jammed. Each leader of a tour group was yelling at top voice, trying to be heard over the shouting of his neighbors, while the tourists themselves all peered heavenward like so many Rhode Island Red hens drinking water. Did the Americans among them clutch to their breasts the erudite tomes about the Sistine ceiling that were for sale in the book stall outside? No way. They clutched *The Agony and the Ecstasy*. It was direct and readable. It was without malice. Though it would not enlighten teachers of art history, neither did it falsify history, and it brought to millions—that's right, millions—of readers more information about Michelangelo and his times than they would otherwise have had. It was for that and not for his historiography that Irving Stone was decorated by the Italian government.

Another way to deal with actual places and people is to cloud their identities by changing their names. The town of Taos, New Mexico, for example, became La Oreja in Frank Waters' symbolic, thickly romantic *The Man Who Killed the Deer*. Lucien Maxwell became Jean Ballard in Harvey Fergusson's *Grant of Kingdom*. The town of Ouray, Colorado, became Argent in my mining novel, *Red Mountain*. (I actually did write a novel once upon a time.) These changes don't fool anyone familiar with the subject, but they do serve as a kind of mumbo-jumbo to hold carping critics at bay. If one complains about errors of fact, the author need only say, "I wasn't writing about Ouray and its early-day rambunctious characters. I was writing about places and people *similar* to them, so go away and let me handle the drama as my narrative demands—a narrative which, after all, has its own kind of truth."

This device is legitimate, I think—*up to a point*. But when the clouding is used to falsify, that is something else. As examples, let us consider two very good books by two very good writers, *Death Comes for the Archbishop* by Willa Cather, and *Angle of Repose* by Wallace Stegner.

The protagonist of Cather's novel is a real person, Jean Marie Lamy of France who, after the American seizure of the Southwest, replaced the bishop of Durango, Mexico, as the administrative head of the Catholic Church in the conquered area. The theme of the novel has to do with the inherent goodness and innocence of a humble, ignorant people eking out hard lives under the luminous skies of New Mexico. Unhappily, these good people, isolated from their old bishopric of Durango by hundreds of desert miles, had fallen under the control of a handful of mostly inadequate local priests. Father Lamy's problem, in both fact and fiction, was to bring about necessary reforms while simultaneously shifting the allegiance of New Mexico's Spanish-speaking clergy to their new American political and ecclesiastical superiors.

Many things militated against Lamy—vast distances, the suspicions of an ignorant people, and the resistance of a native clergy that did not wish to yield the perquisites it had acquired during decades of neglect by Durango. The most recalcitrant of the priests, in Cather's account, was Padre Antonio José Martínez of Taos.

Father Lamy's name is changed, in the novel, to Father Jean Marie Latour, presumably so the author can escape from what I have called "the tyranny of facts." The name of her antagonist, however, remains unaltered—Antonio José Martínez—presumably because Miss Cather felt he deserved the castigation she was about to administer.

Lamy—or Latour, if you will—goes to his first meeting with Martínez filled with dire tales. The priest, he hears, was the instigator of the Taos Rebellion of 1847 during which several Americans, including Charles Bent, just appointed as the first Governor of newly conquered New Mexico, were killed. Seven Indians from Taos pueblo were charged with the murders. According to Miss Cather, Martínez agreed to help the accused in exchange for deeds to their land and then he calmly let them die. He was also guilty of other immoralities. Local gossip, as relayed to us by the author, said he had debauched a fifteen-year-old girl who, aided by miracles, had preserved her virginity during seven years of Indian captivity, but who was helpless in the hands of Padre Martínez.

Martínez' features, as described by Cather, bore out his reputation—shoulders like a buffalo, an egg-shaped face, yellow eyes, and "full lips thrust out and taut, like the flesh of animals distended by fear or desire." He openly told Latour, still according to Cather, that "celibate priests lose their perceptions. No priest can experience repentance and forgiveness unless he himself falls into sin." He added, "Rome has no authority here," and warned his superior not to attempt reforms in Taos. A modern TV soap opera could hardly establish a more titillating conflict. But how much accuracy did the author sacrifice for the sake of drama?

Antonio José Martínez was born into a moderately well-to-do family in northern New Mexico on January 7, 1793. His wife, whom he married when he was nineteen, died the following year in childbirth. Disconsolate, he went to a seminary in Durango to study for the priesthood. There he gulped down the philosophies of liberalism with his theology.

In the mid-1820's he was permanently assigned to the Taos parish. Convinced that education was necessary for a democracy, which Mexico had declared herself to be on gaining independence from Spain, he opened New Mexico's first school, supporting it out of his own pocket. Though his primary interest was steering bright boys into the priesthood, he also invited girls to attend. Twenty of his male pupils took their first steps toward the priesthood in his improvised schoolhouse, but the only one mentioned in *Death Comes for the Archbishop* is a stupid, lazy, greedy, lascivious lout who is rumored to be Martínez' son, sired after the father was ordained.

Because textbooks, missals and catechisms were difficult to obtain, Martínez went to Santa Fe, bought the only printing press in New Mexico, and brought it back to Taos to compose books for his students. He also used the press for printing the first newspaper west of the Mississippi, *El Crepúsculo de la Libertad,* The Dawn of Liberty. The paper died for lack of paid subscriptions, but Martínez found other uses for the press. In 1843 he printed an inflammatory pamphlet charging that American traders whose posts stood close to the New Mexico boundary were trading guns and liquor to the Indians in exchange for buffalo hides and stolen livestock. By destroying the herds of buffalo on the plains, the priest pointed out, the Indians were shortsightedly depriving themselves of their major source of food, and by raiding New Mexican ranches they were increasing the misery of the nation's northern provinces. He urged government action against the traders.

Martínez' chief target was Charles Bent, one of the owners of Bent's Fort on the Arkansas River. Bent, who had married a New Mexican woman, lived much of the time in Taos. There he and his "American Party" of traders and trappers warred constantly with Martínez for control of the northern districts. The priest generally won. He had his brother Pascual chosen Justice of the Peace in Taos over Bent's candidate, and was able to block Bent, for a time, from obtaining through the government part ownership in huge grants of land close to the border. Bent despised him, called him "the Calf"—I suppose because in Bent's eyes he made his living by sucking on the teats of the church—and dripped scorn on Martínez' alleged drunkenness and physical cowardice.

Bent's associates, notably Ceran St. Vrain and Kit Carson of the American Party in Taos, always believed that Martínez fomented the postwar revolt in which the new Governor was killed. Their opinions filtered down through standard Yankee histories to Willa Cather, who either did not learn about or else ignored the report of an official investigative tribunal that cleared Martínez of all charges.

A military dictatorship was imposed on New Mexico following the Taos uprising. While it lasted, very few Spanish-speaking residents of the defeated territory were appointed to offices of any sort. There were some 60,000 people in New Mexico at the time, enough to qualify the territory for American statehood. Hoping that recognition as a state would bring freedom, opponents of the military system called for a constitutional convention and elected Martínez president of the body. The movement failed, but the priest kept struggling, serving three terms in the legislative assembly, only to see the "American party" succeed in establishing a territorial form of government that guaranteed their control of the political stronghold for years to come.

During those years Martínez also warred with Lamy over the Frenchman's replacement of the beloved, hand-carved wooden *santos* and *bultos* in their little adobe churches with tinsel-and-china religious statuettes mass-produced in the East. They quarreled over tithing. Before the conquest, Martínez had led a successful fight to abolish the payments because they were a hardship on his poor parishoners. Lamy ordered tithing restored, partly so he could go ahead with his consuming ambition: the building of a great cathedral in Santa Fe. Outraged, Martínez wrote intemperate letters to the Santa Fe newspapers, charging Lamy with selfishness and greed. When he refused to retract, he was excommunicated.

State government versus territorial government. Tithing versus voluntary contributions. Wooden santos versus china saints—the bickering dragged on and on. Such social and cultural conflicts grow intricate and dull. Consequently, Willa Cather yielded to her dramatic instincts and substituted for history a kind of antagonism that could be more readily understood. That,. even more than her slandering of an intensely loyal patriot, is her sin. She glossed over history. She obscured the true nature of the difficulties involved in the working out of an accommodation between the vanquished Hispanic peoples of the Southwest and their American conquerors—a problem whose intricacies have not yet wholly disappeared. Yet she could not make those tyrannical facts disappear forever. Thanks to the work of several Hispanic scholars, Antonio José Martínez is slowly emerging as an authentic folk hero. Perhaps he even deserves a novel as good as and far more truthful than the one in which he now stands traduced.

For another case of distortion, and a harder one for me to deal with, I would like to turn to Wallace Stegner's *Angle of Repose*. *Angle of Repose* is based of the life of a Victorian gentlewoman, Mary Hallock Foote, and her husband, Arthur D. Foote. Mary Foote was a talented writer and magazine illustrator of the nineteenth and early twentieth centuries. Her natural circle, so she felt, was the coterie of intellectuals and beautiful people, as we might call them today, who revolved around Richard Watson Gilder, editor of the famous old *Century Magazine*, and his artistic, scintillating wife, Helena de Kay Gilder.

Mary Hallock lost this stimulation when she married Arthur Foote, a mining and irrigation engineer. As women did in those days, and to a large extent still do, she went where her husband's work took him—

to New Almaden, California; to Leadville, Colorado; to Mexico; and, most important, to the Boise area of Idaho, scene of several large irrigation projects.

Mary Foote always resented her intellectual deprivations. Her longings created continual tensions in her marriage. Arthur Foote's nature complicated the problem. He was mulish, taciturn, hard-working, scrupulously honest, and possessed of a positive genius for accepting jobs on projects that promptly failed, generally through no fault of his own. Often the family lived on his wife's earnings as a writer and artist, and this dependency bruised her husband's pride. During the long, losing struggle to keep the Boise project afloat, he drank too much—another cause of acidic recriminations. To top off the troubles, Mary Foote endured miscarriages, insomnia, loneliness, and nagging worries about the future of those children who did survive.

As Mary Foote's need for money became less desperate, her production dwindled and so did her vogue. By the 1950's she was known only to a few graduate students groping around for a subject on which to hang a thesis. And then along came Wallace Stegner.

I will now indulge in a little guessing. Stegner has long been interested in that period of the West when engineers, often sponsored by the government, were rushing around locating natural resources for quick exploitation by developers. As a graduate student at the University of Iowa, he wrote a thesis in 1935 on Clarence Dutton of the Powell Irrigation Survey. Now notice: Dutton was the man who hired Arthur Foote, Mary's husband, to work on the Idaho sections of the survey. Later, in 1954, Stegner published *Beyond the One Hundredth Meridian*, an intellectual-cultural biography of John Wesley Powell himself. Among the people who pop up in that book's densely packed pages is the brilliant mining engineer, James Hague. Hague was married to Arthur Foote's sister—that is, he was Mary's brother-in-law.

What I am saying is that it was quite natural for Stegner to have encountered during the course of his researches the reminiscences that Mary Foote wrote in the 1920's when she was about eighty years old; she lived to be ninety-one. What I am guessing is that, having stumbled across the reminiscences, he immediately saw in them the seed of a compelling novel. He took it over—the conflicts, the chronologies, striking figures of speech, literary allusions, whole blocks of descriptive writing, at which Mary Foote excelled, and even the title *Angle of Repose*. Angle of repose is a term used by civil engineers to describe the maximum slope at which pebbles, rocks, or any loose material will stand without sliding. Mary Foote in her reminiscences makes figurative use of the term when comparing her life to a rolling pebble questing for a place to stop. Stegner's title implies exactly the same thing.

One other source of material needs mention—five hundred detailed, intimate letters that Mary Foote poured out, in her loneliness, to her friend Helena de Kay Gilder. These letters are at Stanford University and were available to Wallace Stegner who until recently taught creative writing there.

Having decided to make fiction out of this mass of unpublished material, Stegner came up against the tyranny of facts. What was he to do about names? For some reason, he kept place names as they were, but changed personal names. Mary Hallock became Susan Burling. (Burling, incidentally, is a real and familiar name in the Hallock family tree.) Arthur Foote became Oliver Ward. Thus Mary Hallock Foote was transformed in the novel into Susan Burling Ward. James Hague, the Gilders, and others were similarly disguised.

Of particular importance to our tale is a handsome young engineer, a graduate of MIT, Harry Tompkins, Jr. As a matter of fact, Tompkins came into the Foote's life in Idaho. Stegner, however, names him Frank Stevens, brings him into the story during the Wards' Leadville phase, and makes him a most attractive person—brave, loyal, resourceful, and capable of talking to Susan Ward (i.e. Mary Foote) about novels, poetry, and art, something her husband couldn't do.

Dozens of passages lifted bodily from Mary Hallock Foote's actual reminiscences make identifications unmistakable. Here, for one example, is a short excerpt from Foote's autobiography, *A Victorian Gentlewoman in the Far West: The Reminiscences of Mary Hallock Foote.* "No one remembers Kuna. It is a place where silence closed about you after the bustle of the train, where a soft, dry wind from great distances hummed through the telegraph wires and a stage road went out of sight in one direction and a new railroad track in the other." And here's what Stegner put into a letter he says was written by Susan Ward. "I wish I could make you feel a place like Kuna. It is a place where silence closes about you after the bustle of the train, where a soft dry wind from great distances hummed through the telegraph wires," and so on, word for word. After pages of such echoes, what is the point of changing the peoples' names? I truly don't know.

The book does contain one invented character. He is the narrator, Lyman Ward, identified in the novel as Oliver Ward's grandson. As far as I can determine, Arthur Foote—renamed Oliver Ward—had no grandson. He did, however, have at least two granddaughters and both were alive when *Angle of Repose* was published. That too has its significance in what follows.

The story, as the sorely crippled narrator uncovers it, moves ahead as relentlessly as a Greek tragedy. We are given strong hints that Susan Burling and Augusta Drake were subliminal lesbians. If a literary sleuth reads the letters Mary Foote actually wrote Helena Gilder with that in mind, he can find oblique support for that supposition. But the two women were high-minded Victorians and perhaps did not recognize their own feelings. Or perhaps they were simply very devoted friends, as it was possible to be in those more innocent times. In any event, both married, and the book becomes a study of Susan's adventuresome marriage—an unworkable marriage, mostly because her husband's character was so completely different from hers.

Very gradually, and under the combined stresses of propinquity and deep unhappiness, Susan Ward and Frank Stevens succumb to temptation. Do they succumb all the way, as the soaps have it—or do they indulge only in despairing hugs and kisses? The narrator says he doesn't know. It doesn't matter. While they are hugging or whatever in a nook in the sagebrush beside an irrigation canal built by Oliver Ward, his and Susan's five-year-old daughter wanders off, falls into the ditch, and drowns. Pretty harrowing. So harrowing that Frank Stevens, crushed with remorse, later puts a loaded pistol in his mouth and pulls the trigger.

Okay, what are the facts? There is no indication that Mary Foote ever made love with Harry Tompkins. But I suppose she might have. However, two things very definitely did not happen. Harry Tompkins, the Frank of the novel, never committed suicide. And little Agnes Foote—incredibly, the child is named Agnes both in fact and in fiction—never drowned—she died in her teens from a ruptured appendix.

Stegner did not distort history, as Willa Cather did in *Death Comes for the Archbishop*. Rather, he captured on paper, among other things, one of our nation's deep cultural splits—the values of the materialistic West, with its challenges to engineering creativity, and the East's efforts to establish a base for more traditional and no less compelling standards. To me the book that resulted is a beautifully crafted, densely textured story revolving around skillfully realized characters.

To cloud the characters' identities, he changed their names, just as many writers have done, including Willa Cather—and me. But having changed them, he all but compelled us, by verbatim excerpts from their works, to see them as real people and not as "similarities," which is the heart of the mumbo-jumbo I mentioned earlier. Recognition complete, he then slanders them cruelly—there simply are no other words for what he does—in order to smite the reader with a powerful but wholly fictitious conclusion.

Is this a legitimate exercise of a novelist's powers to create—and to destroy?

Rather than answer, I'll ask another question. Stegner's book won the Pulitzer Prize for 1971. At that time his sources were known only to a few people, and I suppose he thought they would stay obscure. But in 1972 the Huntington Library published Mary Hallock Foote's reminiscences, edited by Rodman Paul. At that moment Stegner's extensive borrowings—one might call them plagiarisms—and his calculated distortions became clear for everyone to see because of his own crystal-clear identifications. I have often wondered what he thought when Paul's book came to his notice, as it quickly did.

For that matter, I wonder what William Shakespeare thought when, in one of his so-called historical plays, he made a diabolical murderer out of King Richard III, when in reality the monarch seems to have been a conscientious and decent ruler.

BIBLIOGRAPHIC NOTES

Willa Cather's information for *Death Comes for the Archbishop* (New York: Alfred A. Knopf, 1927), came primarily from William J. Howlett's eulogistic biography, *The Life of the Right Reverend Joseph P. Machebeuf* (Pueblo, Colorado, 1908), who was Lamy's long-time assistant and supporter; and from Ralph E. Twitchell's six-volume *Leading Facts in New Mexico History* (Cedar Rapids, Iowa: Touch Press, 1912), a thoroughly Anglicized view. As a corrective she could have, but didn't, consult Pedro Sanchez's short biography, *Memories of Antonio José Martínez* (Taos, 1903). Sanchez's account was translated into English by Guadalupe Baca-Vaughn (Santa Fe: The Rydal Press, 1978).

Other balanced accounts of Martínez have since been published at widely spaced intervals in the *New Mexico Historical Review*: C.V. Romero, "Apologia of Antonio José Martínez" (1928); E.K. Frances, "Padre Martínez, a New Mexico Myth"

(1956); Ralph Vigil, "Willa Cather and Historical Reality" (1975). Books treating the milieu in which Martínez moved are George Sanchez, *Forgotten People, A Study of the New Mexicans* (Albuquerque: University of New Mexico Press, 1967); Nancie Gonzales, *The Spanish Americans of New Mexico, A Heritage of Pride* (Albuquerque: University of New Mexico Press, 1969); Frances Swadish, *Los Primeros Pobladores* (Notre Dame, Indiana: University of Notre Dame Press, 1974). Also valuable is Carlos Ramirez' doctoral dissertation, "Hispanic Political Elites in Territorial New Mexico" (Santa Barbara: University of California, 1975).

Pages 150-250 *passim* in Paul Horgan's admiring *Lamy of Santa Fe* (New York: Farrar, Straus & Giroux, 1975) cover the turbulent, complex and confusing post-conquest years that Willa Cather shied away from, though they were integral to her story. (There are several other books about the same decade that searchers for minutiae about the parts played by Lamy and Martínez during those same tempestuous years can look up for themselves.)

My own *Bent's Fort* (New York: Doubleday & Co., 1954) gives Charles Bent's version of his struggle with Martínez. (Consult index.) My sources were the manuscript letters Bent wrote Manuel Alvarez, U.S. Consul in Santa Fe, during the pre-conquest period. The letters were later published sporadically (1954-1957) in the *New Mexico Historical Review.*

Bibliographic data on Wallace Stegner's *Angle of Repose* (Garden City, New York: Doubleday and Co., 1971) are self-evident. One need only read the novel itself and then Mary Hallock Foote's own reminiscences as edited by Rodman Paul, *A Victorian Gentlewoman in the Far West* (San Marino, California: Huntington Library, 1972). See especially Paul's introduction. See also Chapter Five of Richard Etulain's *Conversations with Wallace Stegner on Western History and Literature* (Salt Lake City: University of Utah Press, 1983).

Juan R. García teaches history at the University of Arizona. He has written two books on the experiences of Mexicans in the United States in the twentieth century.

JUAN R. GARCÍA

HOLLYWOOD AND THE WEST: MEXICAN IMAGES IN AMERICAN FILMS

The images that American society has of Mexicans and other Hispanics are deeply imbedded in our psyche, history, literature, and mass media.[1] Unfortunately, many of them have been negative. Since the turn of the century, Mexicans have been depicted in the movies as evil, decadent, primitive, vengeful, licentious and brutal beings with few, if any, redeeming qualities. This trend was set during the early years of filmdom when the Edison Company produced *Pedro Esquivel and Dionecio Gonzales: A Mexican Duel* in 1894. This forty-foot film showed two Mexicans fighting to the death with knives. Thereafter Mexicans became a staple in many of the silent films, often serving as vile bandits and renegades who murdered, plundered, raped, robbed, and cheated. To match their despicable personalities they were saddled with the odious label of "greaser," further revealing the innate prejudice toward Mexicans. Since its early years Hollywood has repeatedly depicted Hispanics as gross, contemptible creatures. Seldom has the industry portrayed Hispanics as individuals with redeeming qualities who, like others, have struggled long and hard to survive.[2]

While the celluloid Mexican stereotype is as old as the industry itself, it should be noted that it was not Hollywood or the movies which created these images. True, such images have been fostered and perpetuated by the medium of film, but Hollywood has received and drawn many of its ideas about Mexicans from history and American

75

literature. Historically, many of our contemporary stereotypes about Hispanics are deeply rooted in the early struggles between Catholic Spain and Protestant England.

As part of its propaganda campaign against Spain, England fashioned a view of the Spanish as being singularly decadent, corrupt, indolent, cruel, primitive, violent and deceitful.[3] Such characteristics are evident in the wood carvings of de Bry which show Spaniards in the process of dismembering Indians, or Catholic priests burning heretics at the stake. That they were capable of such barbarism was given added credence by the writings of Father Bartolomé de las Casas who graphically described the Spanish destruction of the Indian inhabitants of the Caribbean region. Seizing upon his works, Spain's enemies used them to further denigrate Spain and its people. These attitudes and misconceptions were transplanted to the New World and applied to the denizens of Spanish America and their descendants. Anti-Spanish and anti-Indian attitudes were widespread in the early literature about the New World, as exemplified in the following passage written by the Abbé Raynal in 1770:

The ruin of that world is still imprinted on its inhabitants. They are a species of men degraded and degenerated in their natural constitution, in their stature, in their way of life, and in their understanding, which is but little advanced in all arts of civilization.[4]

In describing Latin men and women, Raynal and those of like thinking were perhaps the first to write the basis of most Hollywood scripts about Latins. Literary and scientific works also described the men of South America as weak, impotent, and insecure, and definitely as being no match for the advanced or civilized Europeans. "In the savage the organs of generation are small and feeble. He has no hair, no beard, and no desire for the female. His sensations are less acute, and yet he is more cowardly and timid."[5] Yet, in spite of these shortcomings, Europeans were cautioned against the volatile Latin temperament, which was disguised under his surface pacificity. Later, Hollywood would make sexual incompetence, cowardice, timidity, barbarism and vengefulness trademarks of the Mexican bandidos, thus further perpetuating the Black Legend.[6]

While the tendency was to depict Latin males in unsavory terms, early writers and observers were careful to note that Latin women were different. Unlike their male counterparts, Latin women were often described as sensual and exotic. They were also attributed with an inner strength lacking in Latin males, which made them more courageous and determined in the face of adversity. It should be noted that many of these savants of the Age of Enlightenment had never approached the shores of the New World and thus much of their work was based upon exaggerated, inaccurate and second-hand information. They did not understand the history, people and culture about which they wrote. In the twentieth century the same might be said of Hollywood scriptwriters, producers and directors, as they continue to place the dated misconceptions of the Middle Ages and the Enlightenment on the screen.

The attitudes and stereotypes engendered by the Black Legend became incorporated into American myth, history and literature as the United States came into conflict with Latins in its drive to the Pacific. In the 1830's the Alamo became a symbol of American courage and Mexican brutality and deceit. The Mexican American War of 1846-1848 served to bolster America's image of itself as a powerful, progressive nation which had easily defeated a backward and decadent people. The incursion of explorers, trappers, traders, adventurers and military personnel into the Hispanic borderlands provided Americans with new glimpses into the "strange and exotic" people of the region. Diaries and reports described the hostile climate and environment of the region. They also contained vivid and largely critical descriptions of the mores, values and culture of the inhabitants. Although not widely read or circulated when first written, these accounts later formed the basis for many of the literary and historical works on the Southwest.

Developments in the latter half of the nineteenth century also served to fan anti-Mexican and anti-Hispanic attitudes. The unprecedented growth and development of the United States at this time created tensions within the social fabric of America. It was a time of profound and troubling change as the forces of industrialization, urbanization and immigration altered the face of American society. Those who perceived these forces as posing a threat to traditional American values sought to restore the United States to its pristine past. Included in this group were lay and religious leaders who sang the praises of America's greatness and called upon Americans to rediscover their sense of mission. The era also fostered a virulent nativism which manifested itself in a growing intolerance of foreigners and minorities. To bolster patriotism, loyalty, and pride, the literature of the era once again struck the chord of Anglo-Saxon superiority. While the nostrums found in the literature and sermons helped allay some of the fears and uncertainties, they did not eradicate the anxieties that characterized the Gilded Age. Increasingly, Americans looked Westward in their search for answers and reassurance. In time the West came to symbolize a new world, filled with opportunities and a chance to reaffirm the traditional American values of self-reliance, democracy and progress. In the popular mind the West became a new Eden awaiting settlement and regeneration. Implicit in this view was the idea that the West was a virgin land populated by unregenerated Mexicans and Indians. As Americans began to "settle" the West, a new history and mythology was created in the imagination of writers which would serve to bolster American pride and sense of worth at the expense of Mexicans and Native Americans.

Hollywood has borrowed heavily from this popular literature, which emerged in the form of dime novels from Eastern publishing houses between 1875 and 1925.[7] In dime novels the emphasis was not in achieving balance or accuracy, but on sales and entertainment. Because of tight production schedules, dime novelists relied on standardized plots and stock characters. This resulted in the perpetuation, reinforcement and, to some extent, the creation in the popular mind of images which collectively labeled all Mexicans and Hispanics as undesirables. In most story lines Mexicans became gross caricatures who ran the gamut from the sandal-footed peon to the proud but impoverished hidalgo who clung tenaciously to a bygone era. Between these two extremes were a host of other stock characters, including the evil and scheming priest; the beautiful and strong-willed señorita; the dark and lascivious female half-breed; the jealous but inept Latin lover; and the ruthless and treacherous bandido. All of these literary stock characters were incorporated into the early films, as Hollywood found in their midst a "convenient villain."[8] The popularity of Mexicans as adversaries both in the literature and the movies lay in their appearance, dress, language, culture and religion, all of which stood in sharp contrast to that of the Anglo protagonists. These unidimensional Mexican characters were usually the victims of their own foibles and shortcomings, thus assuring their defeat and/or humiliation at the hands of the fair-haired hero.

As in the case of popular literature, the West became a staple of Hollywood from the very outset. Westerns appealed to filmmakers because the West remained a strange, exotic, yet intriguing place to audiences. Few had experienced the West first-hand, and yet most were familiar with its legends and mythology. The West, with its vast and open expanses, loomed larger than life on the screen. It was beautiful and majestic, but danger and death lurked everywhere in the form of vegetation, animals, weather and inhabitants. The code of the West became survival of the strongest. In the early Westerns individual courage, savvy and determination were seen as desirable and necessary for individual survival. Civilization existed, but only on a precarious level.

Although the West was harsh and unbending, it was also comprehensible. Its laws and codes were simple and direct. One was either right or wrong, good or evil. Justice was swift out of necessity. There was little time or inclination to scrutinize things closely. Time and the elements precluded such malingering. While this was quite evident to the folk heroes who traversed this vast landscape, Hollywood filmmakers wanted to make sure that their audiences understood and accepted this code as well. To place audiences on an equal footing with the protagonist, Hollywood utilized common literary strategies to help them discern the "good guys" from the "bad guys." The strategies used to identify "good Mexicans" from "bad Mexicans," for example, involved the use of skin color, language and oral hygiene. Thus the darker the skin, the more evil and sinister the Mexican. Closely associated with skin color was the villain's inability to speak proper or understandable English, which underscored his stupidity and backwardness. Particularly loathesome or vile Mexicans were furnished with rotten teeth. Mexican bandidos were often amoral characters, dark and sinister in appearance, who placed little value on life. Unrestrained by the mores and rules governing civilized society, they exacted a heavy toll in life and property before meeting their end. Mexican bandits were portrayed as lazy, violent, licentious, cowardly, drunkards, inept, dull witted, vengeful, and treacherous. To underscore their sub-human qualities, they often lacked names. In addition to the term "greaser," they were also commonly referred to as "Mexes," "Mexikins," "breeds," and "mongrels." This was reflected in the titles of some of the early films which featured Mexican bandits, such as *Tony the Greaser,* *Bronco Billy and the Greaser, The Girl and the Greaser, The Greaser's Revenge, The Half-Breed's Treachery, The Mexican's Revenge,* and others which portrayed Mexicans in all kinds of unflattering ways. Movies also depicted Mexicans as spending inordinate amounts of time and energy in attempting to violate lily-white heroines. Fortunately for the heroines, stalwart heroes like "Bronco Billy" Anderson or Tom Mix usually appeared in the nick of time to dispatch the villain before they ruined the heroine's honor. In some cases, when no male hero was about, Anglo-Saxon womanhood was forced to fight off the advances of lecherous Mexicans. Usually the villain was shot or scared off with a weapon. However, in some cases a more novel approach was used, as in the 1912 film *Under Mexican Skies*, wherein the Anglo heroine warded off a "lustful half-breed" with a crucifix.

Even though most of the early Westerns relied heavily on Mexicans as the villains, a number of films attempted to show that they could make the transition from villain to hero. Thus in the 1909 film *A Mexican's Gratitude*, a Mexican bandit undergoes a change of heart when he recognizes that his victim was a man who had saved him from a lynching years before. A few films such as *The Thread of Destiny* (1908), *The Two Sides* (1912), *The Mexican* (1914), and *The Last Resort* (1912) attempted to show Mexicans in a realistic and compassionate light. However, they were few in number and their characters still exhibited many of the heavy-handed stereotypes about Mexicans.[9] By the beginning of World War I, American audiences had become conditioned to the idea that Mexicans were untrustworthy, sadistic, lustful and vengeful. Adding to this view were the strained relations between Mexico and the United States, the violence of the Mexican Revolution, and xenophobia, all of which were capitalized upon by filmmakers. The result was that, "For most citizens living in the population centers of the East and Midwest, the distorted caricatures on the moving picture screen served as their only contact with the culture of Mexican-Americans. While some producers attempted a more balanced approach, these were too few to counteract the adverse image being created by the rest of the industry."[10]

After a brief hiatus during World War I, when Hollywood turned to the nefarious and insidious activities of the Germans, filmmakers once again returned to the use of Mexicans as evildoers and bandits. Yet the war and the problems plaguing relations between Latin America and the United States led to some Latin nations assuming a strong stance against the renewed use of Latin stereotypes. In 1919, for example, Mexico began to formally protest the misconceptions and distorted stereotypes which American movies propagated. In a formal letter to producers, the Mexican government complained about films which depicted its country and people as backward and barbaric. It warned that it would restrict the filming of motion pictures there if the practice continued. When Hollywood failed to heed this warning the Mexican government banned all films which portrayed Mexicans unfavorably. This ban went into effect in 1922.[11] Mexican officials realized, however, that simply banning all films which portrayed Mexicans unfavorably would have little impact, since such films could still be distributed to other countries without the loss of much revenue.

Therefore, it decided to carry the matter one step further and ban all films by companies which produced movies offensive to Mexicans. This, and the fact that other Latin American countries began following Mexico's lead, forced Hollywood to reconsider its policies.[12] Yet Hollywood was loathe to give up one of its most popular villains, and so it resorted to subterfuge in an attempt to get around the new policies. Instead of using locales in Mexico and Central America, film companies moved to Argentina and Brazil. Thus, rather than eradicating the stereotypes, the Mexican restrictions only served to " . . . move the standard Latin American stereotypes to a new location."[13] Another ruse employed by Hollywood at this time was to create mythical cities and nations. It mattered little, for Mexican bandits remained the same. Only the locales and their names were changed.

By the end of the 1920's the Mexican bandit almost disappeared from films, and with him so did many of the Latin themes. In the 1930's Hollywood made fewer Westerns as it focused more upon musical extravaganzas and the so-called "social problem" films. With the advent of Franklin D. Roosevelt's "Good Neighbor Policy," and World War II, Hollywood, at the urging of the federal government, began producing films that attempted to depict the positive side of Latin America. In this respect Hollywood produced some noteworthy, if flawed films, such as *Bordertown* (1935) and *Juarez* (1939). In 1943 and 1945 Walt Disney produced *Saludos Amigos* and *The Three Caballeros* in order to promote good will between the United States and Latin America by portraying its Southern neighbors in positive terms.

In the Westerns, however, Latins continued to fare poorly. For example, the Depression era brought with it a series of Anglo Good Samaritan films in which the protagonist now fought on behalf of innocent and defenseless Mexicans. This was the storyline in films such as *In Old Mexico* (1938), *Song of the Gringo* (1936), and *South of the Border* (1939). These movies helped reinforce the stereotype of Mexicans as people who were unable to help themselves. A similar theme appeared in the gay caballero series, which featured *Zorro* and *The Cisco Kid*. Beginning around 1919 and continuing until 1950, the Cisco Kid series depicted the protagonist as an amorous, charming brigand who prized beautiful women. Cisco, portrayed as a daring caballero, was well dressed and educated. Hint of a high birth and intellect was given by providing him with impeccable manners and a good grasp of the English language. Unfortunately, his erstwhile sidekick Pancho was portrayed as coming from humble origins. His poor English and buffoonery stand in stark contrast to the hidalgo image of Cisco. Yet even Cisco was subject to subtle forms of discrimination in Hollywood. In spite of his breeding and background, his status as a serial hero and Hollywood taboos precluded him from marrying the Anglo heroine. This was not unique to the gay caballero character since the mixing of races on the screen was, and remains, largely unacceptable to filmmakers. However, there is one case in which the gay caballero did get the girl. In *California Conquest* (1952), Don Arturo Bodega (played by Cornell Wilde) joins Fremont's Freedom Forces and helps defeat the "unsavory" Mexicans in that Pacific province. When he pops the question to his bride-to-be, the heroine responds to his proposal by saying: "You would give a lot to be an American, wouldn't you?"[14]

Even when played for humor, the gay caballero series was not very flattering to Mexicans. In *Beauty and the Bandit* (1946), Gilbert Roland plays an amorous brigand who pursues a staunchly independent Anglo heroine. Most of the humor is at the expense of the Mexicans, who are depicted as child-like simpletons. Even Roland's band is laughable as they appear lost without his leadership and direction. The ultimate insult is delivered when the heroine visits their camp and "introduces" them to soap and bathing. As they gather around to look at the bar of soap, they are simultaneously fascinated and repulsed by it. One of the gang members looks at it curiously and says something to the effect that he has heard about soap before but has never seen it.

Another popular character which emerged during the 1930's and which ultimately supplanted the gay caballero in popularity was the so-called "dark lady" or Mexican spitfire. Raised from a minor role to star billing by such performers as Lupe Velez, the Mexican spitfire often displayed a broad mix of emotions on the screen. She usually possessed a fiery temper, great courage, and deep passion with a heavy dose of unreasonableness. Ultimately, however, her erratic behavior was designed to endear her to audiences, especially when her tantrums led to amusing difficulties with the English language. Velez, who starred in eight of the spitfire movies, epitomized the image and tragedy of the "dark lady." When there were no Anglo heroines around it became possible for the dark lady to win the Anglo hero's heart. But if she encountered female Anglo-Saxon competition, she was sure to go down in defeat. Velez, who was born Guadalupe Velez de Villalobos in San Luis Potosi, Mexico, in 1910, became a standard in Hollywood spitfire movies. During her short life she had a tempestuous love affair with Gary Cooper. Cooper loved Velez, but his mother was opposed to the relationship. When it ended Velez met and married Johnny Weismueller. Later she had an affair with actor Harold Ramond. When she became pregnant by him, she felt ashamed that her condition was brought about by a man whom she believed had no love for her. Her last film before her suicide, ironically enough, appeared in 1947 and was entitled *The Mexican Spitfire's Blessed Event.*[15]

Another Hispanic actress who began her career as a dark lady was Margarita Carmen Cansino. She appeared in a number of "Three Mesquiteer" movies which featured trios of cowboys. In 1937 she appeared in her last dark lady film, *Hit the Saddle.* That year she married Edward Johnson, a shrewd businessman who transformed her from a raven-haired dark lady into an auburn-haired sophisticate. Rita Cansino changed her name to Rita Hayworth and by the 1940's had become one of Hollywood's "Love Goddesses." In describing the dark lady character, Arthur Petit writes:

. . . by far the most popular type of dark lady is only half-Spanish and therefore must undergo a long apprenticeship before joining the Saxon hero. These tests of loyalty invariably require the dark lady to desert her race, her native country, or both. Dozens of films exploit her precarious position. She may fall in love with a captured American and rescue him from imminent execution. . . . Perhaps she must turn against a member of her family—a brother, as in *Chiquita, the Dancer,* or a father, as in *His Mexican Sweetheart*—thus demonstrating both her loyalty to the hero and her allegiance to "the land of the free." Whatever the variations on the theme, the outcome is the same. The dark lady gains the hero only by renouncing her past.[16]

In the Westerns produced during the Great Depression and after, Mexicans continued to be portrayed as bandidos and clowns—but also as avengers. Of the three, the avengers often displayed a strength that made them both manly and moral. Although only a few avenger films have been produced, they do offer a welcome respite from the heavy-handed stereotypes associated with Mexicans. The Mexican avengers often "ride in righteous wrath against Saxon oppressors," displaying a single-minded determination to vanquish their adversaries.[17] The avengers also possess a quiet dignity that never falters even in the face of death. This is the case of "The Mexican" in the *The Ox-Bow Incident* (1943). As the story unfolds, three men are captured and accused of murdering a cowboy. "The Mexican," as portrayed by Anthony Quinn, is one of the accused. In the movie Quinn remains nameless, thus underscoring the contempt with which his character is held. Yet Quinn does not passively accept his fate and he definitely is no coward. He attempts to escape, but is wounded in the process. Injured, he asks for a knife so that he can dig the bullet out of his leg. Bartlett, one of the captors, is opposed, saying, "Don't give him no knife. He can throw a knife better than most men can shoot." Quinn responds: "Better than most of you." After digging the bullet out and cauterizing the wound, the "Mex" defiantly and expertly throws the knife so that it lands within an inch of one of the other men's boot. As the other two captured Anglos plead for mercy, the "Mex" refuses to beg, thus helping to dispel the idea that all Mexicans are cowardly. In fact, Quinn objects to being hanged in the company of cowards. After confessing his sins to the only other Mexican in the posse, he goes to his death with dignity.

The actions of "The Mexican" held forth a promise that perhaps Hollywood would begin to counter the offensive stereotypes of Hispanics by producing more avenger films. Yet the Mexican avenger character raised a number of difficult questions and problems, including who his adversaries would be, with whom would he join forces, and his eligibility to court Saxon heroines. Unwilling to resolve these questions, Hollywood produced few successors. For the most part, Mexicans continued playing villains and buffoons who proved no match for the Anglo hero. This is evident in movies such as *Red River*, *Vera Cruz*, *Rio Lobo*, and *Cowboy*.

In the 1960's and 1970's, more sophisticated versions of the Mexican villain emerged. One version has the same bandido character, except that the new bandidos are more competent, expressive and dangerous. The second version involves the half-good bandido who plays a morally ambiguous role in films. A case in point is Tuco, played by Eli Wallach in *The Good, the Bad, and the Ugly*.[18] By the end of the movie, Clint Eastwood has disposed of Lee Van Cleef and has the drop on Tuco. Eastwood then strings up Tuco and leaves him hanging precariously on a wooden cross in the cemetery. At the last moment Eastwood turns in his saddle and shoots the rope, thus freeing Tuco to enjoy the gold that all of them have been pursuing. The film emphasizes the importance of quick thinking, quick acting and technical skills in winning and surviving. The characters, both brown and white, are largely amoral.

Also appearing in the 1960's and 1970's were the "team Samaritan" movies such as *The Magnificent Seven* (1960). In this film we have the elements discussed above. There are the seven gunmen who ride in to save a beleaguered village in the name of justice, compassion and twenty dollars. The seven gunmen constitute an interesting group. One of them is Bernardo O'Reilly (played by Charles Bronson), who is a half-Irish, half-Mexican gunfighter. A second member of the group is played by Horst Buchholz, who portrays a young Mexican farmer who is attempting to conceal his ancestry. The good/bad villain in the movie is Calvera (Eli Wallach), a man of humor and some pretensions who brooks no opposition from the villagers. Calvera also has his own code of ethics that includes protecting the villagers from other marauders and providing for his own men. As for the villagers, they are dressed in the typical white pajamas which have characterized them in countless Hollywood films. They are men who live in fear and resentment of Calvera, but are determined to stop him and free themselves from his raids. After the arrival of the seven, these humble men begin to learn how to defend themselves against Calvera and ultimately help defeat him, wherein they too emerge as honorable and courageous men. Not only is the village changed by the experience, but so are the gunfighters. O'Reilly, who has served as the moral mouthpiece of the story, is fatally wounded in the final scenes. As he looks around at the villagers defending themselves with makeshift weapons, he gives the children around him a final admonition: "See your fathers now!" He then asks, "What's my name?" "Bernardo! Bernardo!" cry the boys. "You're damn right!" answers O'Reilly before dying with a grin on his face. Arthur Petit has written:

The seven were a necessary catalyst, but their example has borne fruit. In the future the villagers will be able and willing to protect themselves. And in death, O'Reilly inverts a major traditional fictional stereotype by affirming his Mexican heritage.[19]

There is no denying that *The Magnificent Seven* has its flaws, including its paternalistic approach to the Mexican character. Nonetheless it does contain some Mexican characters who play roles of crucial moral significance. Yet *The Magnificent Seven* is more the exception to other team Westerns which again rely on traditional stereotypes in depicting their Mexican characters.

Another Western which has enjoyed wide popularity among filmmakers is the Western set in revolutionary Mexico. These movies feature individuals who are rapidly being displaced by the arrival of civilization. Self-reliant, quick on the draw, and still imbued with the code of the West, these individuals find themselves caught in a time warp where many of the old values and virtues have become outdated. Yet there remain a few places where their talents are still at a premium and it is to these places that these men travel for a final showdown with destiny. Unlike the early (1911-1974) Westerns set in revolutionary Mexico, which rarely took ideological stands, the more contemporary films have at times attempted to focus upon the issues, personalities, and struggles of the Revolution. Usually such films tend to favor the revolutionaries against the corrupt *federalistas*. However, when all is said and done, most of the films depict the rebels as being just as repulsive and decadent as the establishment they are combatting. Thus, we have the paradox wherein Hollywood applauds the principles of the Revolution, while disparaging and denigrating the revolutionaries. This ambivalence is in part attributable to the fact that the Mexicans are forced to compete with Anglo soldiers of fortune or mercenaries. Initially the Anglos ride to Mexico to help the rebels. When actions demonstrate that the rebels are not worthy of their help, these individuals turn their backs on both sides and decide to fight independently for their own goals. This is evident in films such as *Viva Villa!* (1934), which features an over-fictionalized account of Pancho Villa's life; *Villa* (1958), wherein Charles Bronson plays Villa's heartless lieutenant who shoots prisoners while he eats breakfast; and *They Came to Cordura* (1959), which provides an inaccurate portrayal of Pershing's Expedition into Mexico.

In essence Hollywood has produced only two or three respectable movies about the Mexican Revolution. One such movie is *The Professionals* (1966), wherein four seasoned adventurers are hired by a Texas tycoon to rescue his wife from the Villista revolutionary Jesus Raza, played by Jack Palance. Predictably, these men must overcome overwhelming odds in order to rescue the "Mexican Marquesa." This they accomplish, but as they return with the tycoon's reluctant wife, Burt Lancaster (whose character had fought in the Mexican Revolution) is forced to shoot a "soldadera." As it turns out, the woman that he shot used to be his mistress. This raises doubts in Lancaster's mind about turning against his former comrades. In time the bandit/rebel Jesus Raza, who is pursuing the professionals, manages to convince them that they should renounce the tycoon's reward and return the wife to her people, with whom she really wants to be in the first place. Petit argues:

Despite its streak of sentimentality, and for all Raza's dependence on the good will of the Samaritan four to regain the marquesa, *The Professionals* is still one of the few 'revolutionary' movies in which the bandit/rebel actually wins the heroine from a Saxon rival, fights courageously, and survives beyond the fadeout. In a real sense Raza is the film's victor."[20]

In 1969 the controversial Sam Peckinpah filmed *The Wild Bunch*. It features four supernannuated gunmen, who after perpetrating a bank robbery and slaughter of citizens in Texas, flee into revolutionary Mexico. It is then that the Revolution begins to control the action and dictate the fate of each of the men.

From the moment the Wild Bunch crosses the Rio Grande, Peckinpah takes special care to set up the rival Mexicans, each symbolized in three ways: by a single person, by a group of persons, and by a place. On the one hand there is the good, natural Mexico, represented by the Villista village, by the Villistas themselves, and especially by Angel (Jaime Sánchez), the Villista member of the Wild Bunch. And then there is evil, unnatural Mexico, represented by the sadistic federal officer Mapache (Emilio Fernandez), by the Mapachistas, and by the squalid town of Agua Verde, Mapache's base.[21]

It is Angel who serves as the voice of his people and cause, and who converts the Anglo mercenaries. Mapache's execution of Angel serves as ". . . the catalyst for both the physical destruction and the moral resurrection of the Wild Bunch."[22] The final scenes of the film are graphically violent as the remaining members of the "Bunch" wreak havoc on Mapache and his people. These sequences are disturbing in a number of ways. Not only does the film continue the practice of perpetuating Anglo superiority by depicting three men who literally wipe out hundreds of armed Mexicans, but it also has them failing to make a distinction between those who deserve to die and those who do not. As a result, we witness not only the slaughter of Mapache's men, but also of innocent women, children, and elderly people. This bloody and violent ending, according to Petit, is designed to make the moral point that there are two Mexicos—one represented by the evil Mapachistas and the other represented by Angel and his people. Mapache and his men, in Peckinpah's eyes, perverted the Revolution and thus had to be destroyed. The Villistas, on the other hand, represent the unfulfilled promise of the Revolution. Yet Peckinpah is not convinced that Mexico has been cleared of people like Mapache. There will be others to replace him and ultimately it will be this faction that will prevail.

Perhaps the best film about the Mexican Revolution was Elia Kazan's *Viva Zapata!* (1952). Unlike Peckinpah, Kazan presents a more favorable and optimistic view of the Revolution and its participants. The film does have its flaws, in that it possesses historical inaccuracies, fallacies and stereotypes. Yet Gary Keller believes that it " . . . is the most comprehensive and attentive Hollywood film ever produced about the Mexican Revolution."[23] The film does not contain Anglo Good Samaritans, mercenaries or heroes, and this makes it unique. The focus is upon Zapata, the Mexican people, and the ideology of the Revolution. It deals with moral questions and the conflict within Zapata, who finds himself in the unenviable position of a man who is not quite of the people but who eventually joins them in their struggle. In the end Zapata is assassinated, gunned down in a flurry of bullets. His magnificent stallion escapes into the mountains and, as the villagers gather around the bullet-riddled body, one of the *campesinos* spits and tells the other that the dead man is not Zapata. The real Zapata, he says, still rides in the mountains and will continue to fight for the people. "The film's finale," according to Gary Keller, "is an accurate and highly moving one. It apotheosized the peasant leader as an enduring example of rebellion, a hero whose values can be relied upon by the *campesinos* in future times of need. The warnings in *Viva Zapata!* against power apply equally to the extremists of left-wing revolution and right-wing reaction. The film not only interprets the past, but foreshadows events that have since occurred."[24]

Films such as *Viva Zapata!*, however, are more the exception than the rule. For the most part, Hollywood has preferred the "greaser" bandido, the Mexican buffoon, the dark spitfire or the fearful peasant in depicting Mexicans or other Hispanics. The tradition continues to the present day, as reflected in 1983's *Barbarosa* starring Willie Nelson and Gary Busey. In one scene featuring a Mexican cantina, every stereotype imaginable is depicted, ranging from the greasy bartender, to a man with bad teeth, to the Mexican "whores" who fight over Busey.

Another continuing tradition is to have non-Hispanics play Hispanics in such films. Given Hollywood's caste system, it is unlikely that the characterizations or the actors who portray them will change. It seems to be a commonly held belief that if more Hispanic actors and actresses were given important roles in these films that things might change. Perhaps so. But it will require them to be major stars and to challenge roles that denigrate Hispanics. Some efforts toward creating a positive image of Latins have been undertaken by actors such as Ricardo Montalbán who in 1969 formed NOSOTROS, an organization devoted to protesting stereotypes and improving the image of Hispanics in Hollywood films. In 1978 the Los Angeles Chicano Cinema Coalition was founded in order "to promote the growth and development of a Chicano cinema aesthetic" and to work toward social justice.[25] In a related vein, independent Chicano filmmakers have begun to produce films that seek to portray Hispanics in a more realistic and favorable manner. While some, like *The Ballad of Gregorio Cortez* (1982) have received critical acclaim, they have not done well at the box office. Most moviegoers are not interested or accustomed to seeing "good Mexicans" against bad and evil Anglos. Racism and prejudice make people uncomfortable, especially if those perpetrating them are Anglo. Most moviegoers appear more interested in being entertained than enlightened and sensitized.

Therein lies the major concern about the Latin images which flash across the screen, for Hollywood has occupied a central role in the perpetuation of unseemly Hispanic stereotypes. True, film is escapist fare designed to entertain audiences and its effect might not be so nefarious if there was something to counteract and counterbalance these largely negative images. Yet there is very little to balance the scales. The result is that most Americans, including Hispanics, derive from the film industry a distorted, troubling and frightening image of Hispanics, their culture and their place of origin. What viewers have been repeatedly presented with is a view of a Latin society populated by murderers, bandidos, cowering peasants, violent and amoral revolutionaries, erotic and loose women, and people living in filth and squalor. Such images reinforce existing fears, suspicions and hostility toward Hispanics. At times they manifest themselves through mass deportation drives or through proposed legislation which seeks to ban further entry of people from Mexico and Latin America in an effort to protect the United States from the social, economic and political maladies attributed to the people of these countries. In the United States, such images and stereotypes are used to justify or rationalize exploitation, discrimination, and prejudice against Hispanic Americans. They create further barriers to mutual respect and understanding between people.

There is little to offset these stereotypes in other arenas. For example, the press usually dwells on the negative aspects of Latin American society, choosing to emphasize revolutions, economic distress, the smuggling of drugs or undocumented workers, or rampant corruption. On occasion newspapers and magazines have gone so far as to warn Americans against travelling south of the border because of the dangers that await them. Americans read few if any scholarly and accurate works on Latin America, thus most of the information they receive about Hispanics comes from the media and the Hollywood film industry. Because of this, Hispanics continue to be victims of the stereotypes that they have fought against for so long.

The movies have long mirrored our fears, hopes, dreams, and anxieties. In many ways they are more reflective of our society than they are of the people and places they depict. If this be so, then the movies represent a barometer by which we can measure not only the place which Hispanics occupy in American society, but also how they have fared in it.

ENDNOTES

[1]This paper is an enlarged version of Professor García's presentation at the OLD SOUTHWEST/NEW SOUTHWEST Conference, "From Zorro to Zoot Suit: The Latin Image in American Films."

[2]Blaine P. Lamb, "The Convenient Villain: The Early Cinema Views the Mexican-American," *Journal of the West*, XIV, No. 4 (October 1975), pp. 75-81.

[3]For an informative discussion about the origins of these attitudes see: Charles Gibson, ed., *The Black Legend: Anti-Spanish Attitudes in the Old World and the New* (New York: Alfred A. Knopf, 1971); Philip Wayne Powell, *The Tree of Hate: Propaganda and Prejudices Affecting United States Relations with the Hispanic World* (New York: Basic Books, 1971).

[4]Abbé Raynal, *Philosophical and Political History of the Settlements and Trade of Europeans in the Two Indies* (1770-1772), cited in Allen L. Woll, *The Latin Image in American Film* (Los Angeles: UCLA Latin American Center Publications, 1977), p. 3.

[5]Raynal, p. 4.

[6]The Black Legend was a term coined in 1906 by Julian Juderais, a member of the Generation of '98, to describe anti-Spanish attitudes and beliefs which served to denigrate Spain and its people.

[7]For a discussion of how Mexicans were depicted in the popular literature and the dime novels see Juan R. García, "The Mexican in Popular Literature, 1875-1925," in *Down Mexico Way* (Tucson:

Arizona Historical Society, 1984), pp. 1-14.

[8]Lamb, *passim*.

[9]Lamb, p. 79.

[10]Lamb, p. 80.

[11]Woll, p. 17.

[12]Woll, p. 19.

[13]Woll, p. 19.

[14]Gary D. Keller, "The Image of the Chicano in Mexican, United States, and Chicano Cinema: An Overview," in *Chicano Cinema: Research, Reviews, and Resources* (New York: Bilingual Press, 1985), p. 29.

[15]Keller, p. 30.

[16]Arthur G. Petit, *Images of the Mexican American in Fiction and Film* (College Station: Texas A&M University Press, 1980), p. 142.

[17]Petit, p. 142.

[18]Although *The Good, the Bad, and the Ugly* was produced in Italy by Sergio Leone, it was distributed in the United States by United Artists, where it brought in large box office receipts.

[19]Petit, p. 218.

[20]Petit, p. 224.

[21]Petit, pp. 231-232.

[22]Petit, p. 233.

[23]Keller, p. 36.

[24]Keller, p. 37.

[25]Jesús S. Treviño, "Chicano Cinema," *The New Scholar*, 8 (1982), p. 176.

WILLIAM EASTLAKE

THE FAILURE OF
WESTERN WRITING

This conference is about "regional" Southwestern writing. The problem is, there is no such thing. Literature is never merely regional. If it's called literature, it must be universal.

There is much writing about this region, and, oddly enough, the first of what we call regional writing about the West was done by people who never left New York City. The books were called dime novels, later pulp novels, then "slicks." Regional film writing about the West was written by Hollywood writers who thought America was a blank space between New York and Hollywood.

When people who lived in the West began to write about the cowboy, a strange thing happened. The writers in the West saw their country not as it was, but as the Eastern writers conceived it. When they deviated from the script, their New York editors told them their books would not sell. There is truth to this. The readers had been corrupted by the New York publishers to expect a fake West, and reality disappointed them. The fake myth became reality to the reader.

Why did the genius writers of America reject the West? Herman Melville, instead of adventuring to the West—his own mythic country—decided to search the South Seas. Mark Twain spent much time in the West, but went to New England to write about life on the Mississippi. Stephen Crane of *The Red Badge of Courage* visited the West and promised to write about it and live out his old age as a cowboy, but fled instead to England where he died at the age of twenty-six. The great American poet, Walt Whitman, saw the West as the American promise, but stuck it out in New Jersey.

Why did writers like Mark Twain repudiate the West? Did they find that the purpose of the Westerner was to kill off the Indian and make a quick dollar? The Chambers of Commerce and the land developers were not Walt Whitman's idea of achieving the American dream. The West had no time for the artist. The fake myth was good for business.

We can see the fakery at work in Tombstone, Arizona, today, and in Tucson there are people who remember when the town was part of the beautiful desert, crisscrossed by a few dirt roads. Now Tucson has become a traffic jam, a bomber base, and a maker of weapons to destroy this small planet. Tucson is a recapitulation of the old West, a West based on war and the making of a fast buck, the West that sent writers like Mark Twain back home to achieve his genius. If peace were declared, Arizona would be out of business.

Oscar Wilde, on his trip West, thought that the power and magnificence of the Rocky Mountains and the vast stretch of an endless country subdued the artist, and it sent him back home. Nature said, according to Wilde, "Look, look, I can create better than man can." This same Oscar, when asked by the American customs inspector what he had to declare, answered, "Nothing but my genius." But that genius, like our American geniuses, found very little to write about in the West.

If the past has failed us, what about the present crop of writers? We must keep in mind that the only criterion for genius is survival value. Which of the present writers will be around a hundred years from now—if our planet lasts that long?

We must keep in mind that selling well is no sign of endurance. An acquaintance of mine wrote a book for the University of California about all the best-sellers, many of which sold millions of copies. Most of their authors are unknown today. Does the bad writing tend to push out the good writing? There is evidence that it does. If readers don't get what they like, they'll learn to like what they get. The publishers will see to that.

As more and more publishers become the property of conglomerate oil companies, the chances of a book of quality being published become limited, and are rapidly becoming nonexistent. As book stores become chains, there is less and less chance of a literate manager selling books of merit. So the writers in our Southwest find themselves—if it is any consolation—in a universal situation: starve or teach.

William Eastlake came to the Southwest from New York in the 1950's. His novels about this region have been printed in nine languages.

But, we have to ask ourselves, what about the potential writers who attend these universities? What universities did our great writers attend? Mark Twain's university was a Mississippi steamboat, digging for gold, and the brothels of San Francisco.

Herman Melville's university was a four-masted sailing ship cruising the South Seas.

Walt Whitman's was the Civil War Union hospitals of the dead and the dying.

George Orwell's university was being down and out in Paris and London, a Burma adventure, and enlisting as a common soldier to fight fascism in Spain.

Steinbeck's university was a ranch in California and a Dust Bowl in Oklahoma.

Hemingway's university was any war he could find.

And Faulkner, after being kicked out of "Ole Miss" for flunking English, found his university shoveling coal in a power plant. These are the schools our geniuses came from.

Now that so many potential writers attend formal universities, what is happening to them? Can creativity be taught? I suspect you can lead a student to water, but you cannot make him think. I teach occasionally, and find that the best you can do is to encourage those who show a spark—what Thomas Wolfe of *Look Homeward, Angel* and *Of Time and the River* called a "flash."

The best teacher is life—don't waste it. The best school is your local library—use it.

My university was a run-down ranch I bought in nowhere in northern New Mexico between the Apache and Navajo reservations, at eight thousand feet elevation, where forty below was common. I restored the ranch with the help of the Indians and made a living from it running cattle. That accomplishment meant more to me than any satisfaction I got from my writing, although I suspect that that joy of true accomplishment must have shown in my writing—particularly in my book, *Portrait of an Artist with 26 Horses,* and my other New Mexican novels.[1]

How important is a sense of place? A writer should develop his characters out of a long familiarity with place so that place becomes part of his unconscious, that part of the brain where all good writing comes from.

I never wrote about Indian country until I had become a working part of the place.

I never wrote about the wars I have been involved in until sufficient time had elapsed for the unconscious to take over. In Vietnam I was a correspondent for a magazine, and I didn't have to write for a deadline, and that was helpful. (Does working for a newspaper help or hurt a writer? Stephen Crane and Ernest Hemingway found a short newspaper career helpful—but for God's sake, keep it brief.)

Again—we should not think of ourselves as Southwestern writers, but only as writers who happen to live in the Southwest.

Dostoyevski did not think of himself as a Siberian or a Crimean writer.

Or William Shakespeare as a Stratford-on-Avon writer.

Labeling a writer as being from a region can be hurtful.

Walter Van Tilburg Clark told me his first book, *The Oxbow Incident*, was handled by his publisher as a Western. In those days a Western sold for $2.50 and a so-called standard book for about $3.50. By accident, *The New York Times* reviewed his book as a non-Western and other journals began to take the book seriously—so the publisher changed the book jacket and raised the price.

I have this problem continuously with my publishers. They want a shootout on the jacket covers of my books. Readers who are used to the traditional Westerns are disappointed by my books. And the reader who would appreciate a non-Western view of the Southwest relegates the book to a Western and does not buy it. However, I am fortunate that most of my books are still in print in this country and in foreign translations. But I think we should keep this in mind about a writer's survival value: if we are not writing for *our* time, we may not be writing for *any* time.

Perhaps the Western novel will not succeed until the novelist who happens to live in the West will think of himself as an artist, as does the composer and the painter. As an artist who sees his country with a third eye. As James Joyce saw Ireland, as Picasso saw his subjects as cubes, as Van Gogh twisted his landscapes. They all gave us a strange insight into reality. Nonfiction shows us what is seen with two eyes; fiction gives us a third eye.

The problem is, the audience does not want a new vision. We fear new insights. The artists I've mentioned all went through long periods of rejection. The modern writer wants instant success, needs immediate applause.

My friends who write for TV make huge sums and their residual payments go on for years. There is small money in attempting to write well, so the writer who lives in the Southwest has the same obstacles that are universal, with an added handicap that the reader expects the book to carry on the tradition of the fake West, the cliché writing that is the only writing he understands. The hack writer has devoted his life to doing something badly that has been done far worse before.

Those who try to write well can get a small satisfaction from the fact that my classical composer friends have a much tougher time of it. It costs a small fortune to form a symphony orchestra to give you a hearing. And the painter is faced with a great problem, too, in trying to get a New York gallery to give him a showing, when trash sells so well.

My friends who try to write well cannot fail. They have a shot at attempting the impossible. Some never get past the small literary magazines; some remain unpublished, as Van Gogh in his lifetime remained without a sale, but they have the excitement of attempting discovery, of going to a place where no one has been before.

Perhaps the writer has no choice. Freud thought a person was doomed at an early age to conform to a pattern, so that perhaps a writer has only an imagined say over how he will write. We like to think we have some control over our destiny in spite of the clinical evidence.

I think we do. We must try. And fail. And try again.

I called this essay "The Failure of Western Writing." It might better have been called "The Failure of Writing in Our Time." Although I happen to live in the Southwest, if I lived in the East, the South, or the Far West, I would be conscious of our failure there.

I want to stress that it's important for a writer to use all the experiences of his life in his work. Not just write about his immediate environment—which in my case is the Southwest. While working on my ranch, I found it a change of pace to write a novel, which I called *Castle Keep*, based on my experiences in the Second World War. The castle was an ancient chateau I occupied during the German Ardennes offensive that brought back to me all the memories of the dead and the not-so-dead and all the American poetry of army language.[2]

Columbia Pictures did not find the army language amusing or poetic. They found it obscene. Simon and Schuster did not find it obscene. I was fortunate to have a former army man as my editor there, so it was the first book published by a large publisher to print army language.

I found all war books prior to my effort to be false, including such classics as *War and Peace*. Fake, because the obscenity of army language is universal—a reaction to the obscenity of war and the outrage against the civilians who sent the soldier to his coming death. Typically,

Norman Mailer's war book contained euphemisms which any ex-soldier found ridiculous. (Columbia Pictures with Burt Lancaster and Peter Falk did a cleaned-up film version of *Castle Keep*, to my disappointment.)

I later left my ranch and went off to the war in Vietnam as a correspondent for *The Nation* magazine. Out of that came my novel, *The Bamboo Bed*. The book sold well in Europe, but not too well here. I suspected at the time that not many wanted to be reminded of our disaster.

Stephen Crane wrote that there are only two things worth writing about—cowboys and Indians, and war. I had the good fortune to write about both, although I do not agree with Crane. I suspect there must be something else worth writing about. But I find that, through circumstances, these have turned out to be my favorite themes.

Will I go off to Central America to be witness to another American tragedy? I do not think so, because I fear it will be another repeat of Vietnam. America solved its problem with England through war, with the Mexicans through war, with Spain through war, made numerous invasions of our southern neighbors—all victories. War has become the great problem-solver, including Vietnam.

In Vietnam the native Vietnamese became the American Indians, as I attempted to show in *The Bamboo Bed*.

The grave-registration chopper came in low over the remains of Clancy's outfit. Everyone on Ridge Red Boy to Mike seemed very dead. They were quiet as lambs. Sometimes you could only see what looked like smoke coming up from a fire but it was only ground fog. Everyone with Clancy was dead. All the Alpha Company. It was the biggest thing since Custer. Mike, who called himself a correspondent, had to watch himself. You tended to take the side of the Indians. You got to remember that this is not the Little Big Horn. This is Vietnam. Vietnam. Vietnam. They all died in Vietnam. A long way from home. What were the Americans doing here? The same thing they were doing in Indian Country. In Sioux Territory. They were protecting Americans. They were protecting Americans from the Red Hordes. God Help Clancy.

You could tell here from above how Clancy blundered. Clancy blundered by being in Vietnam. That's a speech. The chopper circled now low over the dead battle. Clancy had blundered by not holding the ridge. Clancy had blundered by being forced into a valley, a declivity in the hills. It was the classic American blunder in Vietnam of giving the Indians the cover. The enemy was fighting from the protection of the jungle. You couldn't see them. Americans love the open. Americans do not trust the jungle. The first thing the Americans did in America was clear a forest and plant the cities.

Concentrate on the battle below. Do not always take the side of the Indians. You could see here clearly from above how Clancy blew it. In the part of the highlands of Vietnam near the Cambodia-Laos bunch-up there is no true open country. Everything is in patches. You could see, you could tell, by all the shit of war, where Clancy had made, where Clancy had tried to make, his first stand on the ridge and then allowed his perimeter to be bent by the hostiles attacking down the ridge. Then Clancy's final regrouping in the draw where all the bodies were. Clancy should have held that ridge at all costs. If you must fight in the open fight high. Then the only way the enemy can kill you is with arching fire. Mortar fire. You can dig in against mortar fire. When they force you in the valley you are duck soup. They can hit you with everything from above. From the way the bodies lie Clancy had mounted three counterattacks to get the ridge back that he had too early conceded. The attacks were not in concert. He did not hit them all at once. There should have been more American bodies on the ridge. Clancy should have paid any price to get back the ridge. The ridge was the only opportunity. The valley was death. Ah, but the valley is comfortable. The hill is tough. And the men are all given out and dragging ass, tired and leaking blood. See where they stumbled up and where shot down. See where they failed. See where they tried again and again and again. Where they were shot down. See the paths of bright they made with their blood. Why is that native killing me? Why Weintraub? Why Clinton? Why Oliphant? All dead. The valley is beautiful, warm, and in this season of Vietnam soft in the monsoon wet. Contemplative, withdrawn, silent and now bepatched, bequilted with all of the dead, alive with scarlet color, gay with the dead.[3]

Regarding the future: The evidence is that a nuclear winter is a distinct possibility. If there is no future, the writer must create one. With a coming holocaust, why should the writer persist? Why should the writer write? Not only because a poet told us to "rage, rage against the dying of the light," but also because another told us, "I have promises to keep and miles to go before I sleep."

After the holocaust, if these few words are found deep amid the rubble, a new species may find of value the following information that I learned from my Navajo neighbors in northern New Mexico and which ended my novel, *Dancers in the Scalp House*:

But the Indians of the Checkerboard Clan, led by the Medicine Man, When Someone Dies He Is Remembered, do not believe that there is a death up there with streets of gold and angels in the big space. The Indian believes that all of everything is continuous on earth—a continuum through nature—so now again it was the time of the cactus-fruit harvest, when the Indians gather tunas, those red-ripe berries, and fruit from the cow's tongue cactus and the beaver tail. It was the time again, too, when they would gather again the pitahaya fruit from the saguaro and the organ pipe. It was also the time again when they would gather wild piñon nuts from the high country. The Indian belief completes a circle, and life comes back on itself, so that there is a continuity in time and place and person. The Indian belief is a circle that recontinues all the rhythms and the poetry of life—so abruptly and alone and together the red canoe rode up the deep and blue river of the undiscovered country, guided by the eagle Star.

The undiscovered country is a perfect wilderness before civilization, before death—around them now a virgin continent abloom with the glory of nature, alive with quick flashing streams, a smogless sky, all the world a dance of light where all was beginning, nothing ever ended, because the undiscovered country is the delight of cold morning sunrise; it is truly the ecstasy and somber fulfillment of the human spirit in watching the sun come down red red redding all in magnificent effulgent blaze from in back of the Sangre de Cristo Mountains. The red snow-drenched mountains. The undiscovered country is the gamboling of the sheep. It is the myriad dancings of the yebechais of Blessing Way, of Healing Way.

The undiscovered country is the crisp mornings and the piñon smoke and the brother sister and peoplehood of all Indians on a July day; it is all the sweetness of infant Navajo babes in cradle boards and the way a coyote looks at you when you talk at him.

The undiscovered country is love and compassion and an inkling into the sufferings of others and the smack of lightning and the tintinnabulation of a small rain on the hogan roof and the joy in the feeling for life. The undiscovered country is not the complications of and dismay at life's problems but the ease and wonderment at life's mysteries. It is the only country that abides.[4]

SELECTED WORKS BY WILLIAM EASTLAKE

[1]*Portrait of an Artist With 26 Horses.* New York: Simon and Schuster, 1963.

[2]*Castle Keep.* New York: Simon and Schuster, 1965.

[3]*The Bamboo Bed.* New York: Simon and Schuster, 1969.

[4]*Dancers in the Scalp House.* New York: Viking Press, 1975.

John Nichols' most famous New Mexico novel, The Milagro Beanfield War, *has been made into a film.*

elson Algren.
⎣: "I submit that
is put to the legal
⎵'

⎣rich Heine, the great
⎣ve on his casket not a
private in the liberation

⎣ an offering from Bertolt
⎣s a weapon."
⎣uthwest, and who often writes
⎣conscience that is in touch with)
endlessly that we in the Southwest
⎣se, my view is not limited to the
⎣ook at the world, the world is in a heap
is only a small part of the world. And
⎣ened deserts from the problems of lower
Nor should we separate Mirror Lake in
⎣g Reservoir up above New York City where
⎣ower. Nor should we separate the southside of
⎣ddle of the Mohave Desert. Because basically all
⎣ents, are undergoing a similar kind of negative
⎣et in general is under attack.

101

In fact, many ecologists and conservationists (not to mention economists, sociologists, and politicians) are pretty much convinced that we may have but fifty years left to get the world back on track. Naturally, the point of view depends on who you talk to. Some folks say fifty years, others say eighty years. A few enlightened doomsayers feel we've only got twenty years before the whole ecological mishpocha will come crashing down about our heads.

So obviously, something has got to be done, and fast, before the damage is irreversible.

Myself, I live in Taos, New Mexico. A quaint and beautiful little town in the Southern Rockies. I've lived there for sixteen years. What I see in the genesis of my own little town is basically a metaphor for the rest of the nation, the rest of the planet. For Taos is locked in a life and death struggle to survive in some kind of healthy and balanced manner. But things are going awry at dozens of crucial levels. All kinds of groups in Taos want to stop the development of the town before it's too late. They wish to preserve the mountains and the forests and the mesa, the rivers and the quality of life. Other groups are working night and day to develop the mesa, deplete water supplies, exploit natural and human resources. Conservationists wish to keep the nearby Rio Grande wild and scenic. Developers would like to make the Rio Grande into a rafters' and vacationers' paradise. So I find that if my conscience is really tickling me a lot, I can probably go to a meeting every night of the week about some aspect of the struggle going on in Taos.

And it never stops. There are no breathers, no allee-allee-in-come-frees. And, like I said, the situation is the same the world over.

One struggle in my town concerns a little river called the Rio Fernando. It comes out of Taos Canyon. About eight miles up the canyon is a development called the Valle Escondido. And in the Valle Escondido are many summer homes for people from out of state who visit Taos for a couple of months each year, in the summer. Unfortunately, the headwaters of the Rio Fernando are in the Valle Escondido, and are used extensively by the developers of this tourist paradise. I say unfortunately, because eight miles below, in the Cañon section of Taos, many small farmers depend on that water to irrigate their crops. But in the middle of summer, when farmers need the water most, tourists up in the Valle are impounding the water for their little trout ponds, and for their golf course. And so the Cañon farmers often get next to nothing for their needs.

And so the farmers have gone to court at least four times in the last thirty years to try and curb illegal water usage by the tourists up above, so that they can irrigate during the summer season. Every time they've gone to court, the farmers have won sympathetic judgments from one water master or another, saying they have a priority right to the Rio Fernando's water. But the problem with these judgments is that nobody enforces them. So each year the problem is repeated. If the farmers want the water that they depend on, they have to fight for it.

One day, some years back, the Valle Escondido developers decided the farmers were so powerless, that they might as well just divert the entire river into their fields and playgrounds. So they bulldozed a dam across the entire river. And not even a drop of water flowed down to Cañon. So the farmers called up the State Engineer in Santa Fe and explained the situation. And the State Engineer said, "Ok, fine, we'll have a special water master sit on this problem and get back to you."

When the farmers asked, "When?" the engineer said, "Well, we can probably arrange it as soon as September."

And the farmers said, "Wait a minute, we need the water now, September is too late."

But the State Engineer replied, "Well, that's as fast as the wheels of justice are going to move on this particular case."

So that night a group of farmers drove up to the Valle Escondido with guns, shot up a couple of bulldozers, got one started, and drove it into the dam. And at ten o'clock the next night, I got a phone call from the developers' lawyer asking me to come to a meeting at the Taos County Courthouse. I went. At the meeting were State Engineer's representatives, Cañon farmers, and various lawyers for the developers. Everybody was in a panic, afraid that a war was about to start, and somebody might get killed. And the upshot was that the developers promised to have that dam out of the river by the next morning—and that is what happened: they bulldozed it out. And the river flowed down to the Cañon farmers so that they could irrigate. And that is one little example of how we made the legal system function on our behalf in Taos.

Like many places in the Southwest, Taos is enveloped in myth. The myth states that Taos is very beautiful and spiritually powerful. It is a wonderful haven for artists and writers, and the air itself is exquisite. The light is exceptional, and perfect for the artist. And the harmony of the valley can enrich the most downtrodden soul. And many people make pilgrimages to Taos, seeking this delightful quality of life.

Unfortunately, there is a wide gap between myth and reality in Taos. True, an artist can hire an Indian from the local Pueblo to pose for a few dollars an hour. Then the artist can turn around and sell the painting for a thousand, two thousand, five thousand dollars. But the man or woman or child who posed for the painting comes from a society where the average income for a family of four is probably around three or four thousand dollars a year; and unemployment is from sixty to eighty percent.

Taos County, in fact, is one of the poorest counties in the nation. It is sandwiched between two other counties, Mora and Rio Arriba, which are even more impoverished. So a different way of looking at Taos is to say it's a very picturesque rural ghetto. And the economics there are similar to the economics of Strawberry Mansion in Philadelphia or Bedford Stuyvesant in Brooklyn. And because of the poverty culture there is an awful lot of misery, crime, alcoholism, and utter frustration among much of the populace.

Taos also has the distinction of being one of the five most polluted areas of New Mexico, after three open pit copper mines, and Rio Grande Boulevard in Albuquerque. Taos gets that pollution from too many cars on undeveloped dirt roads, and from people burning wood. We all burn piñon for nine or ten months of the year; the smoke gets caught in constant inversions. And the particulate matters in wood are probably every bit as poisonous as the particulate matters in bituminous coal.

And seventy percent of the Taos housing is considered substandard; and much of the water supply is polluted because of antiquated well systems, outhouses, and poor drainage.

So at many levels Taos is really not as picturesque as it seems. Its problems of natural and human habitat are as endemic as they are in Third World countries, or in the ghetto neighborhoods of most of our larger cities.

Another scenic river in Taos is called the Rio Hondo. It has the distinction of being the most polluted river in New Mexico. It originates in the Taos Ski Valley, one of the best ski areas in the West. Unfortunately, most people who live downstream in Arroyo Hondo or Arroyo Seco or Valdez, dislike the ski valley because it pollutes their river, and because it is destroying the whole cultural and ecological nature of the area. And for years the residents of these small agricultural communities have waged a never-ending struggle to impose checks and balances on the ski area, in hopes of preserving the integrity of the environment down below where they live.

The litany of battles in Taos, during my time there, has been endless. For ten years the Bureau of Reclamation, the State Engineer, and a number of developers tried to impose a large dam and a lake on the area. The lake would have impounded 12,000 acre feet of water for the "small farmers to use in irrigation." It was hailed as a project "to save a dying culture." But Taos residents soon realized that the water would actually be used more for tourism and municipal development than for irrigation, yet it would be paid for with taxes raised from imposing a conservancy district on all residents of the valley. And marginal people, poor people, small farmers, were actually going to drown in the costs. So the farmers banded together and fought the conservancy district for a decade, and finally got the case thrown out by the New Mexico Supreme Court.

So the process of active struggle to maintain values, culture, and a healthy society has gone on almost every day of the sixteen years I've lived in Taos. In just the last few weeks, I've been attending meetings that concern rafting on the Rio Grande. Six years ago there was no rafting on the river. But now, every spring, there is a deluge of rafters, an out-of-control carnival of tourists floating the river. And this carnival has come to threaten wild and human habitat alike along the Rio Grande in Taos County. The little river town of Pilar, south of Taos, is panicked, because BLM projections for the next three years suggest that as many as 100,000 rafters will use the river. Rafting has become big business, and the Pilar citizens are up in arms because the rafters piss on their lawns, stomp on their vegetable gardens, discard beer cans, and are responsible for rising crime rates. Traffic problems in the enclosed area abound, and the locals are desperate to control the zoo before it gets entirely out of hand, destroying the river, destroying their peaceful village.

Every place you turn in Taos, something else is under attack. For example, I love to fly fish in the Wild and Scenic section of the Rio Grande. Especially I enjoy an area called the Big Arsenic Springs. Not for away, however, is a large molybdenum mine in Questa. And recently the BLM, which manages the wild river section of the Rio Grande, told the moly mine it would be okay for them to build a new tailings pond in a saddle of Guadalupe Mountain, which overlooks the Big Arsenic Springs. And that tailings pond would drain chemical poisons into the river at Big Arsenic, and threaten the fish and other wildlife for miles downstream. So I must attend meetings to try and reverse that irresponsible decision.

Basically, then, if you want to live in an area that retains some kind of human and ecological integrity, you have to fight for it. Particularly if you are a writer, a cultural worker with a voice. I disagree with anybody who wants to run away from the onslaught, seeking some new haven as yet untarnished by human folly. Because every place on earth is either currently threatened, or will soon be threatened. You can't even hide in the Amazon Jungle any more. And so it is important, everywhere, to stop and make a stand: in the countryside, in the cities, *everywhere*.

I remember a Joseph Conrad novel, *Victory*. In it, as I recall, a fellow named Axel Heyst, and his girlfriend, flee to a deserted island, seeking a utopian situation away from the cold, cruel world. But in the end a bunch of nasties from the mainland hear that they've got lucre on their island. And the thugs arrive and pillage the place, and Heyst and his girl are powerless to stop them because they have made no provision to defend their paradise. The moral of that story always seemed to be: you can't run away from society, because society is always going to intrude in the end. So it behooves us all to learn how to hone all the weapons of our creative and positive survival.

One way that I as a writer have tried to participate in the struggle has been to make much of my work overtly political. I consider it advocacy literature. In most of the world the writer is by definition political. You simply cannot separate art from social responsibility in France or the Soviet Union. That's why so many writers outside our borders are suppressed or executed, or wind up living in exile. But here in the United States of North America, there has grown up a myth that being "political" is not "artistic." I think that myth developed most strongly since the McCarthy period of the '50's, during the establishment of the Cold War.

Most recently, a major proponent of the myth has been the Nobel laureate, Isaac Bashevis Singer. He has said that "no Marxist has ever written a good novel." Naturally, I immediately bridled when he said that, because I look at the world from a fairly Marxist point of view. Singer went on to state that a Marxist "has never written a good novel because a writer must have roots, and Marxism is against roots. Marxism is cosmopolitanism, and a cosmopolitan cannot write a good work of fiction—because a writer belongs to his people, to his clan."

When asked, "Do you feel that a writer ought to commit himself in political or social affairs?" Singer replied: "It's unhealthy. I have never seen a single political novel, or a single novel which has to do with sociology, which really came out well. Sociology deals not with a single person, but with masses of people; and in a way this is true of all the sciences . . . ." And he added, "The writers who don't discuss character, but problems—social problems or any problems—take away from literature its very essence. They stop being entertaining."

Which all strikes me as sheer poppycock.

For example, one of the things I tried to do in one of my more popular "Southwestern" novels, called *The Milagro Beanfield War,* was to write about social problems, and also make the book entertaining. And apparently *Milagro* works on those levels. I don't know how many people who read it are aware that *Milagro* is a book about class struggle, or that it's written by a person with a Marxist world view, whose aim is to teach, propagandize, and, ultimately, change the reader's social, economic, and political perceptions of the universe. That was my intention. But if readers had any doubt about where I stood in *Milagro,* my guess is that if they read my follow-up novel, *The Magic Journey,* they probably figured it out. Because *The Magic Journey* is a pretty straightforward book about how capitalism works to a negative effect in America, in any place. It's a book about the destruction of the Southwest, the destruction of Taos—the destruction of the planet—and what ought to be done about it.

And, Isaac Bashevis Singer notwithstanding, I am aware that there is a long and honored tradition of this kind of artistic involvement in the socio-political adventures of history. Let me quote some writers, from this and other countries, on the subject.

Thomas Mann said that "unity of humanity, the wholeness of the human problem, permits nobody to separate the intellectual and artistic from the political and social, and to isolate himself within the ivory tower of the cultural proper."

Jean Renoir, the French filmmaker who wrote and directed *Grand Illusion* and *The Rules of the Game,* said in his autobiography: "Our present day religion is the bank and our language is publicity. The key word is output, by which we produce more. When the world market is saturated we start another war to get new customers. The aim of warfare is no longer conquest but construction. When the building is destroyed, the wheels turn again. We build skyscrapers in the ruins of pagodas and this fills the belly of the working man who would otherwise revolt."

Bertolt Brecht said, "They tell me eat and drink, be glad you have it. But how can I eat and drink when my food is snatched from the hungry and my glass of water belongs to the thirsty?"

And John Reed, author of *Ten Days That Shook The World,* wrote: "All I know is that my happiness is built on the misery of other people, that I eat because others go hungry, that I'm clothed and other people go almost naked through the frozen cities in winter. And that fact poisons me, it disturbs my serenity, it makes me write propaganda when I would rather play."

And the same is very true for myself.

Hans Koning, author of *A Walk With Love And Death* and *The Revolutionary,* put it this way: "If we're to survive against the state, and against Them, we want a constant, a day and night militancy on everything, every single damn issue. Nothing is uncontroversial and nothing they suggest is innocent. Every word is a stone and every plan a barricade. The Bastille has to be retaken every single bloody day. Sounds pretty exhausting and a bore, but what other chance would there be of self-preservation?"

Which brings me to my point about working for the defense of the Southwest. As a writer or an artist, or simply as a concerned citizen, I don't think we can "save" this land by dreaming of better days. I don't think we can do it by walking into the desert and planting a spear and saying "I'm going to make my stand here." Rather, I feel that the only way we can halt the carnage is by taking an active responsibility at many levels for trying to change the nature of our society, our economic system, how it works and who it works for. The fact is that our Southwest, our country, the *world* is dying because the two major concepts of our economic system are Planned Obsolescence and Conspicuous Consumption. Not to mention the appalling and destructive waste generated by a society based almost wholly on the profit motive.

We North American people are only six percent of the world's population, but we consume fifty percent of the earth's resources every year. That's a lot of greed and profit, and it means that not only our own people (and natural resources) but the people and natural resources of the entire world suffer great damage in order to service our absurd and overwhelming needs. And as long as we continue to support such a destructive system, nothing is going to change. And we'll all, good or bad, wind up living in the heartless desolation caused by our rotten habits and extensive needs.

Sometimes I get frustrated, listening to the complaints of our idealists and dreamers about the destruction of the planet. Books like *Bury My Heart At Wounded Knee* are full of beautiful rhetoric about rivers that shall run no more, and how the buffalo were all destroyed. True enough, but most of the gorgeous rhetoric is contained in surrender speeches. And surrender speeches will get us nowhere. Much ecological writing of today is packed with the right-on sensibility of conservationists who bewail the gathering Armageddon, but have no concrete suggestions or solutions for turning the thing around. What's lacking are the guts to understand the power structure doing all this damage, and then rise up and go after it and change it.

For if we don't like what the developers are doing, we have to throw them out, and then come up with viable alternatives. We have to tackle the philosophy that makes it all possible. We have to educate people to the total, complex nature of the destruction. But our gadflies always seem to stop short of this, afraid to really rock the boat. We set ourselves up to fail because we refuse to attack, or take responsibility, for challenging the heart of the problem. Which is the system. Which is hundreds of years of basically unchecked capitalist exploitation—of people, of natural resources.

We lay out all the factors of pollution and human misery, and then too often retreat to whimpering, ineffectual reformist political positions. We admit it's insane to bring water from Alaska, or to float icebergs up the Rio Grande in order to quench the thirst of Santa Fe, but we neglect to take that last step, the active political step, which says we simply cannot continue to support an economic system based on Planned Obsolescence and Conspicuous Consumption.

And why not? Put most simplistically, because those two ideals assume that resources are infinite. And we know beyond the shadow of a possible doubt that this is not true. Therefore, capitalism as we know it and have supported it, cannot go on much longer. Forget communism or socialism, the fact is our society is destroying itself from within. We are by far our own worst enemy. And if we don't rise up and change it at every level, we'll simply eat and consume ourselves into an early grave. And that is why I conclude that any American writer, artist, cultural worker, or concerned citizen involved in our society must take a much more militant and radical attitude about the problems in our society than has heretofore been the norm.

Let me finish here by reading a few more quotations from writers who I think have done a good job at coming to grips with our problems, and forcing us, through their work, to consider tackling things in a more active and militant way.

In *A Continuous Harmony,* Wendell Berry says, "If you are concerned about air pollution, help push for government controls, but drive your car less, use less fuel in your home. If you're worried about the damming of wilderness rivers, join the Sierra Club, write to the government, but turn off the lights you're not using, don't install an air conditioner, don't be a sucker for electrical gadgets, don't waste water. In other words, if you're fearful of the destruction of the environment, then learn to quit being an environmental parasite. We are all in one way or another, and the remedies are not always obvious so they certainly will aways be difficult. They require a new kind of life, harder, more laborious, poorer in luxuries and gadgets, but also I'm certain richer in meaning and more abundant in real pleasure."

Loren Eiseley, author of *The Immense Journey,* wrote in his later book, *The Invisible Pyramid:* "We live in an epic of localized affluences. . . . A few shifts and subterfuges may, with increasing effort and expense, prolong this affluence. But no feat of scientific legerdemain can prevent the eventual exhaustion of the world's mineral resources at a time not very distant. It's thus apparent that to apply to western industrial man the term 'world eater' is to do so neither in derision nor contempt. We are facing, instead, a simple reality to which up until recently the only response has been flight. The flight outward from what appears unsolvable and which threatens in the end to leave an impoverished globe."

In *The Voice Of The Desert,* Joseph Wood Krutch wrote, "Hence it is that even in the desert, where space is cheaper than in most places, the wildlife grows scarcer and more secretive as the human population grows. The coyote howls farther and farther off, the deer seek closer and closer cover. To almost everything except man, the smell of humanity is the most repulsive of all odors. The sight of man the most terrifying of all sights. Biologists call some animals cryptozoic, that is to say 'leading hidden lives.' But as the human population increases, most animals develop as the deer has been developing cryptozoic habits. Albert Schweitzer remarked somewhere that we owe kindness even to an insect when we can afford to show it, just because we ought to do something to make up for all the cruelties, necessary or unnecessary, which we have inflicted upon most of the whole of animate creation. Probably not one man in ten is capable of understanding such moral aesthetic considerations, much less of permitting his conduct to be guided by them."

And finally, let me take this from Aldo Leopold's book *A Sand County Almanac.* "That land is a commmunity is the basic concept of ecology. But that land is to be loved and respected is an extension of ethics. That land yields a cultural harvest is a fact long known but latterly often forgotten. Wherever the truth may lie, this much is crystal clear: a bigger and better society is now like a hypochondriac so obsessed with its own economic health as to have lost the capacity to remain healthy."

Later on in the book, Leopold says: "Man always kills the thing he loves, and so we the pioneers have killed our wildness. Some say we had to do that. Be that as it may, I am glad I shall never be young without wild country to be young in. Of what avail are forty freedoms without a blank spot on the map?"

The problem, then, is obvious. And no writer—or anyone else, for that matter—can any longer afford to ignore the macroscopic overview. Returning to Nelson Algren, we would all do well to remember that "literature is made upon any occasion that a challenge is put to the legal apparatus by a conscience in touch with humanity."

This means that nobody can run away anymore. Beautiful eulogies to "the old days" are ineffective. Desperately seeking wild places to escape to won't turn anything around. We all must labor mightily to understand the overall problem, then educate others about it. This means developing a revolutionary consciousness, and then taking actively to the barricades in whatever ways we deem ourselves most effective, with the dream and the intention of one day seizing power, and moving the colossus in a different and healthier direction.

Only that process of a daily confrontation with the power structure, in our work, holds hope for the future. Or can halt the destruction of the Southwest—or of the entire planet.

BIBLIOGRAPHY

Algren, Nelson. *Chicago: City on the Make,* New York: McGraw-Hill, 1983.

Berry, Wendell. *A Continuous Harmony: Essays Cultural and Agricultural.* New York: Harcourt Brace Jovanovich, 1972.

Brown, Dee Alexander. *Bury My Heart at Wounded Knee: An Indian History of the American West.* New York: Holt, Rinehart, and Winston, 1971.

Conrad, Joseph. *Victory: An Island Tale.* Garden City, New York: Doubleday, Page and Company, 1915.

Eiseley, Loren C. *The Immense Journey.* New York: Random House, 1957.

————. *The Invisible Pyramid.* New York: Scribner, 1970.

Koning, Hans. *A Walk with Love and Death.* New York: Simon and Schuster, 1971.

————. *The Revolutionary.* New York: Farrar, Straus and Giroux, 1967.

Krutch, Joseph Wood. *The Voice of the Desert: A Naturalist's Interpretation.* New York: Morrow, 1971.

Leopold, Aldo. *A Sand County Almanac.* New York: Oxford University Press, 1949.

Nichols, John. *The Magic Journey.* New York: Holt, Rinehart, and Winston, 1978.

————. *The Milagro Beanfield War.* New York: Holt, Rinehart, and Winston, 1974.

Reed, John. *Ten Days That Shook the World.* New York: Boni and Livwright, 1919.

Singer, Isaac Bashevis. *New York Times Sunday Magazine,* Nov. 26, 1978.

Rudolfo Anaya teaches Creative Writing at the University of New Mexico. His most recent work is a novel on Quetzlcoatl.

RUDOLFO A. ANAYA

AN AMERICAN CHICANO IN KING ARTHUR'S COURT

A variety of voices comprise the literature of the Southwest. Writers from each of the cultural groups write from their particular perspective. Eventually these different perspectives will form the body of work we call Southwestern Literature. I say eventually, because as of now the contemporary writings of the Chicano and Native American communities—while they are flourishing—have not yet been widely disseminated and have not yet made their final impact on the region.[1]

It is understood that whenever cultural groups as different as the Anglo American, the Chicano and the Native American exist side by side, cultural sharing takes place; but also each group will develop a set of biases or stereotypes about the other groups. This is unfortunate, but it is a substantiated historical fact. The problem is compounded, of course, when one of the groups holds social, political and economic power over the other groups. Then prejudices will affect in an adverse manner the members of the minority groups.

How do we make the literature of the Southwest a truly multicultural literature which informs the public about the variety of voices which reflect the cultures of the Southwest? Can our different literatures help to lessen the negative effect of cultural stereotypes?

I am an American Chicano, and I have titled my essay "An American Chicano in King Arthur's Court." For me, King Arthur's Court represents an archetypal time and experience in English memory, an archetype transplanted onto American soil by the first English colonists. It is an archetype which is very much alive. (Remember the Kennedy administration reviving the dreams of Camelot?) In other words, King Arthur's Court represents a "foreign" archetype that is not indigenous to the Native American memory.

There is no judgmental value attached to what I have just said. King Arthur's Court has a right to exist in the communal memory of the British and the Anglo Americans. It is part of their history, part of their identity. And communal memory is a force which defines a group. Camelot and King Arthur's Court are "real" forces in as much as they define part of the evolution of this group's eventual world view.

In 1846, King Arthur's Court moved to what we now call the Southwest United States. During the war with Mexico the United States occupied and finally took Mexico's northern territories. In so doing the United States acquired a large population of Native Americans and Mexicanos. Suddenly a very different social, economic and political system was placed over the social system of the Mexicanos. The Mexicanos became Mexican-Americans. A different world view with its particular archetypes was imposed over the communal memory of the Mexicanos. In the area of artistic impulse and creation, this element of the Anglo culture would cause as many problems for the Mexicanos as did the new language and value system with which they now had to contend.

The Mexicano of the Southwest had his own vision of the world when the Anglo Americans came. The view was principally Hispanic and Catholic, but it was also imbued with strains of belief from the Native American cultures. The culture was Hispanic, but in its soul and memory resided not only Western European thought, Greek mythology, and the Judeo-Christian mythology and religious thought, but also the thought and mythology of Indian Mexico. The Mexicano was, with few and isolated exceptions, a mestizo population. Therefore, its world view was biased by the memory of the indigenous, American cultures.

Since 1848, King Arthur's Court has been the social and legal authority in the Southwest. It has exercised its power, not always in a fair and judicious way. My concern here is to explore how the Anglo-American value system affected the artistic impulse of the Mexicano. Did it impede and stifle the creative impulse of the Mexicano, and if so, did it interfere in the Mexicano's self identity and artistic impulse?

The artistic impulse is an energy most intricately bound to the soul of the people. Art and literature reflect the cultural group, and in reflecting the group they not only deal with the surface reality, but with that substratum of thought which is the group memory. The entire spectrum of history, language, soul, voice, and the symbols of the collective memory affect the writer. A writer becomes a prism to reflect those elements which are at the roots of the value system. We write to analyze the past, explore the present, and anticipate the future, and in so doing we utilize the collective memory of the group. We seek new visions and symbols to chart the future, and yet we are bound to mythologies and symbols of our past.

I remember when I started writing as a young man, fresh out of the university, my mind teeming with the great works I had read as a student. I was affected, as were most of my generation, by the poetry of Dylan Thomas, Eliot, Pound, Wallace Stevens. I had devoured the works of world authors, as well as the more contemporary Hemingway, Faulkner, Steinbeck, and Thomas Wolfe, and I felt I had learned a little about style and technique. I tried to imitate the work of those great writers, but that was not effective for the stories I had to tell. I made a simple discovery. I found I needed to write in *my* voice, of my characters, using my indigenous symbols. I needed to write about my culture, my history, the collective experience of my cultural group. But I had not been prepared to explore *my* indigenous, American experience; I had been prepared to deal with King Arthur's Court. I discovered that the underlying world view of King Arthur's Court could not serve to tell the stories about my communal group.

I suppose Ultima saved me. That strong, old curandera of my first novel *Bless Me, Ultima*, came to me one night and pointed the way. That is, she came to me from my subconscious, a guide and mentor who was to lead me into the world of my native American experience. Write what you know, she said. Do not fear to explore the workings of your soul, your dreams, your memory. Dive deep into the lake of your subconsciousness and your memory, find the symbols, unlock the secrets, learn who you really are. You can't be a writer of any merit if you don't know who you are.[2]

I took her kind and wise advice. I dove into the common memory, into the dark and hidden past which was a lake full of treasure. The symbols I discovered had very little to do with the symbols I knew from King Arthur's Court — they were new symbols, symbols I did not fully understand, but symbols which I was sure spoke of the indigenous American experience. The symbols and patterns I found connected me to the past, and that past was not only my Hispanic, Catholic heritage; that past was also Indian Mexico. I did what I had never been taught to do at the university. I got in touch with myself, I explored myself, and found I was a reflection of that totality of life which had worked for eons to produce me.

Each writer has to go through the process of liberating oneself and finding one's true stream of creative energy. For Chicano writers it has been doubly difficult because in the formative years we were not presented with the opportunity to study our culture, our history, our language.

My generation will receive at least some thanks from the future, if only because we dared to write from the perspective of our experience, our culture. Of course a steady stream of Southwestern Hispanic writers had been producing works all along. Before and after 1846, poetry, novels and newspapers were produced, but those works were never part of the school curriculum. The oral tradition was alive and well, and its artistic impulse was invigorating to those of us lucky enough to grow up in its bounty. But by the 1960's the Hispanic culture had reached a crisis point. Not only were the old prejudices affecting us adversely, but the very core of the culture was under threat.

The Mexican American community needed economic and political justice in the 1960's. It also needed an artistic infusion of fresh, creative energy. We had to take a look at ourselves and review a world view which had permeated the culture for hundreds of years. This is precisely what the Chicano Movement of the 1960's and '70's did. The Chicano Movement of those decades fought battles in the social, economic and political arenas, and in the artistic camp. Taking up pen and paint brushes, we found we could joust against King Arthur's knights and hold our own. In fact, we often did extremely well because we were on our soil, we knew the turf. Quite simply, what we were saying was that we wanted to assert our own rights, we wanted to define ourselves, we believed that our world view was as important as any other in terms of sustaining the individual and the culture.

We engaged actively in large-scale production of creative literature. We insisted that the real definition of our community was in the arts, in poetry and stories. A wealth of works was produced which was labeled the Chicano Renaissance. This view of the writers working from within the Chicano community helped to dispel some of the old stereotypes and prejudices. We could think, we could write, we did honor parents and family, we did have a set of moral values, we were as rich and as complex a cultural group as any other group in the country, and so the old, one-dimensional stereotypes begin to crumble.

We explained to the broader "mainstream" culture that we are American Chicanos; we are an inherently American, indigenous people. We are Hispanic from our European heritage, we are Native American from our American heritage. We are heirs to the mythologies and religions and philosophic thought of Western civilization, but we are also heirs to the mythologies, religions and thought of the Americas. A renewed pride in our American heritage defined us.

Out of the Native American world flowed a rich mythology and symbology which the poets and writers began to tap and use. We confronted our mestizo heritage and proudly identified with this New World person. The idea of an original homeland, typified by the concept of Aztlan, became a prevalent idea. The homeland was indigenous, it was recorded in Native American legend. For the Chicano consciousness of the '60's it provided a psychological and spiritual center. One of the most positive aspects of the Chicano movement was its definition of a Chicano consciousness. Spiritually and psychologically the Chicano had found his center, he could define his universe with a new set of symbols, new metaphors. He had tapped once again into his native experience and recovered the important, archetypal symbols of his experience.

That consciousness which was defined in the art, poetry and stories of the Chicano writers continues to exist not just as a historical phenomenon that happened in the '60's and '70's. It continues to define the Chicano collective memory. The power of literature, the power of story and legend is great. True, the Chicano Movement has waned in social action, but the renewed consciousness born in the literature of those decades survives in art, writing, history, and in the language and the oral tradition of the people. In a broader sense, its humanistic principles of brotherhood, its desire for justice, its positive cultural identification, its definition of historic values, and its concern for the oppressed continue to be guiding principles in the thought and conduct of American Chicanos. Chicano consciousness continues to center us, to instruct us and to define us.

The evolution of Chicano consciousness created a new perspective in humanistic philosophy. It took nothing away from our Hispanic European and Mexican heritage, it took nothing away from other Western influences; on the contrary, it expanded the world view of the Americas. But we are still involved in the struggle to define ourselves, to define our community. Evolution is a slow process. Once the definition of Chicano consciousness has worked itself into the society, then we will not have to be so sensitive about the Edenic concept of King Arthur's Court. After all, we understand its right to exist as a mythology, we understand it as part of the definition of a particular group. The challenge for us, for the writers of the Southwest from all cultural groups, is to understand and accept those views which define groups and the individuals from all communities.

Part of our task is to keep reminding each other that each cultural community has an inherent right to its own definition, and Aztlan does define us more accurately than Camelot. Hildalgo and Morelos and

Zapata are as valuable as Washington, Jefferson and Lincoln. The mythology of Mesoamerica is as interesting and informing as Greek mythology. Mexico's settlement of her northern colonies is as dramatic and challenging as the settlement of the thirteen United States colonies. As American Chicanos, we have a multi-layered history on which to draw. To be complete individuals we must draw on all the world traditions and beliefs, and we must continue to understand and strengthen our own heritage. We seek not to exclude, but to build our base as we seek to understand the interrelated nature of the Americas. Our eventual goal is to incorporate the world into our understanding. But in the span of world time, the Chicano community is a young community. It is still growing, still exploring, still defining itself. Our history has already made valuable contributions to American thought and growth and we will continue to make more. What we seek now, in our relationship to the broader society, is to eliminate the mindless prejudices which hamper our evolution, and to encourage people of good will who do not fear a pluralistic society and who understand that, as a group of people define themselves in a positive way, the greater the contribution they make to mankind.

For a century American Chicanos have been influenced by the beliefs imposed by a King Arthur's Court scenario. We have learned the language, we have learned the rules of the game. We have adopted part of the cultural trappings of Arthur's Court, but we also insist on keeping true to our culture. The American Southwest is a big land, a unique land. It has room for many communities. It should have no room for the old, negative prejudices of the past. When we, each one of us, impede the fulfillment of any person's abilities and dreams, we impede our own humanity.

ENDNOTES

[1]This presentation was given in Tucson in October 1984 as part of a lecture series for the Writers of the Purple Sage project. Mr. Anaya's talk at the OLD SOUTHWEST/NEW SOUTHWEST Conference, "The Voice of the Chicano in the New Southwest," continued this theme.
[2]Rudolfo A. Anaya, *Bless Me, Ultima* (Berkeley, California: Tonatiuh-Quinto Sol International, 1976).

THOMAS J. LYON

BEYOND THE FRONTIER MIND

Let me begin with a couple of sweeping generalizations: first, that the qualitative watershed in Western American literature is between the frontier mind and the post-frontier mind; and second, that the distinctiveness of the better regional literature is that it not only describes the ending of a major period in human affairs—the frontier era—but also outlines what it might take, in heart and mind, for us to survive this ending. Thus I am seeing Western literary history not as a purely scholarly occupation but something that might prove more generally instructive.

I want to try to fill out these ideas by concentrating on a few Southwestern nature essayists, because they so forthrightly describe this change in paradigms. When they met the wilderness of the Southwest, the openness and the light and the unmodified character of the land stretching away into the distance may be said to have altered them. Almost their first reaction, or first reflection, was to question the adequacy of traditional ways of seeing. Something was before them for which the received aesthetics, and the received philosophy in general, were no preparation. The remarkable family resemblance among Western nature writers, at deep levels of outlook and value, seems to arise from their having crossed a divide in some ways, and in the new perceptual territory ahead having had strong experiences of a non-fragmented, that is, frontierless world. They bring back an interesting, perhaps significant report.

From the point of view of the frontier mind, which is to say the Christian-Greek-Cartesian-Lockeian dualistic outlook, nature is

119

natural resources. These may be strippable coal, or dammable rivers, or beautiful scenery prepared for by a government sign: "scenic turnout ahead," but the shared characteristic of this kind of nature is that it is the world apart. It is the object of which we are the subject, epistemologically; it is the wilderness where man, in the words of the 1964 Wilderness Act, "is a visitor who does not remain." It is the realm of the instinctual and the unconscious—what we must shape, or rise above, if we are to fulfill our human potential. So said Joseph Wood Krutch in *The Modern Temper* in 1929. He concluded that book with words that seem to sum up the position of an entire civilization: "Ours is a lost cause and there is no place for us in the natural universe, but we are not, for all that, sorry to be human. We should rather die as men than live like animals."[1] To be human is to accept alienation as a basic fact. A year later, in 1930, Sigmund Freud set forth his own reflections on man in *Civilization and Its Discontents*. Again, alienation from nature is seen as a fundamental, structural condition; man channels his nature-given impulses and biological urges into broader, more diffuse social bonds, so that he can band together in what Freud saw as the human project: "going over to the attack against nature and subjecting her to the human will."[2]

Freud, and the early Krutch, seem to have captured the note of heroism that sounds in so much human self-description: given the disjuncture between man and nature, the correct attitude is one of pressing onward. There is perhaps a touch of melancholy or even loss, and neuroses may crop up, but definitively, man is progressive. He is going somewhere; at the least, when he dies, it is as *man*, distinctive. This notion of identity I would call the frontier mind. First among its building blocks, so to speak, is the frontier, the no man's land, between self and other. This first egoism or dualism is repeated and enlarged in "mind" versus "matter," "man" versus "nature," "civilization" versus "wilderness," and so on.

The second element of the frontier mind, logically arising from the first, discomforting, alienated sense, is the felt need for world-changing activity. To the isolated self, existence is a matter of continuing scarcity and insecurity. As far as it can see, it is no longer within the matrix— "there is no place for us in the natural universe." In its need, it is naturally inspired to activity: something is wrong and needs to be changed. But the logic of this particular situation seems to be that whatever the isolated self or species does to secure itself only results, within its consciousness, in a reinforced sense of separateness. Selfhood takes on heroic, tragic dimensions, as a kind of engine is set in motion

Thomas J. Lyon teaches English at Utah State University and is the editor of the journal Western American Literature.

in which needs serially increase, while the world is pauperized to meet these needs. The frontier mind regularly passes through successive frontiers of need-satisfaction, and thus is dulled to the perception of limits. The recognition of limits—that is, the recognition of the limited and ecological nature of the world—would seem to threaten nothing less than the logic of the human project and within that project the ground of identity.

If we agree with Lewis Thomas that preserving this separate identity has been man's "most consistent intellectual exertion down the millenia," and with the economist Kenneth Boulding that "the image of the frontier is probably one of the oldest images of mankind," we begin to see the hardiness of the problem, and the difficulty of transition to a post- or non-frontier orientation.[3]

Most of us, of course, have no burning desire for such change. We surround ourselves with proofs of the rightness of our course. Framed views of nature, for example, as in the windshield sights mentioned earlier, or in much calendar art, correspond with the concept of nature as object, and as part of the collective wisdom give the viewer a pat on the back—he is separate, of course, a "subject," but he appreciates, he is friendly to nature, he is basically a nice guy. Arguably, this position is a step up from not noticing at all—merely running roughshod.

To perceive framelessly, if we could—what would this indicate? John Muir, in the chapter entitled "A Near View of the High Sierra," in his first book, *The Mountains of California*, 1894, describes guiding some painters to a spot in the mountains from which they could do the usual thing: foreground, middle ground, and the rest. He then went on higher, alone, eventually making the first ascent of Mt. Ritter. In a decidedly religious, transformative moment on the summit, Muir gloried in a full 360° view, "laving," as he said, in the "blessed light" and "wide blue sky."[4] As Herbert Smith has pointed out, Muir's account of the two contrasting ways of seeing is a parable of release into the natural world. As such, on the map I am drawing here, it is a trail sign indicating the heart country of Western American literature.

Clarence Dutton, an Army captain and one of the important government surveyors of the nineteenth century, spent parts of the years 1875 through 1881 studying the geology of the Four Corners region. Seeing the Grand Canyon, he was moved to question the received aesthetic traditions, and to denounce the habit of quickly folding such magnificence into categories. "Forms so new to the culture of civilized races [Dutton wrote in *Tertiary History of the Grand Canyon District*] and so strongly contrasted with those which have been the ideals of thirty generations of white men cannot indeed be appreciated after the study of a single hour or day."[5] Time, taking time, letting the landscape have its say, requires setting aside the constant activity and movement, and the urgency, of the frontier mind. A person, Dutton is saying, should open up to the place, rather than instantly starting to manipulate it in some fashion. Dutton's job was, after all, to translate the Southwest into geological language, which of course has conventions of its own, but his stance of respect for the land, the primacy of it, comes through in his descriptions. In a certain way he seems to have been humbled—his stated goal of description became an unadorned, documentary realism. Again in *Tertiary History*, he writes about the Vermilion Cliffs:

There is no need, as we look upon them, of fancy to heighten the picture, nor of metaphor to present it. The simple truth is quite enough. I never before had a realizing sense of a cliff 1,800 to 2,000 feet high. I think I have a definite and abiding one at present [page 56].

The "realizing sense" seems to be the key phrase here, denoting a major change in outlook. Dutton does not say what this "realizing sense" is, exactly, and perhaps such an exposition would be beyond the scope of a government report.

To get closer to the moment, I will turn now to Mary Austin, whose great contribution, arguably, was to codify the inward dimension of the landscape encounter. In many different ways she declared the meeting of mind and land as her own center, and she went so far as to base her faith in the human future on it. Her philosophy was based almost entirely on the incandescent moment when perception suddenly ceases to be dualistic. In that moment the living unity of the world stands forth, changing all relations and values. The moment might occur anytime, even during such a perfectly ordinary event as walking through a stand of junipers:

You walk a stranger in a vegetating world; then with an inward click the shutter of some profounder level of consciousness uncloses and admits you to sentience of the mounting sap.[6]

What you see and feel, when this shutter clicks open, is the "thread of kinship," in Austin's phrase. Her faith is that of the transcendentalist: when you penetrate past the habituated self and are, for however long, not blindered and blinkered by its peculiar needs, what you experience is a beautiful order. Order, and unity. In *Experiences Facing Death* Austin wrote:

. . . at the furthest reach of my individual consciousness, when it achieves for a moment or two the Unitive Life, knowing itself in touch with the Universal, it knows not only the inexpressible, *but knows never so explicitly, it is inseparably a part of all experience, past and to come.*[7] [Emphasis Austin's]

Thus, in the logic of unity, the capacity is in everyone to touch the world at its source and its inherent creativity. In *Everyman's Genius* Austin argued that creativity, or "genius" as she called it, is the general human birthright.[8] This inward fire of contact may be dampened by what she called in *A Woman of Genius* "the huge coil of social adjustment," but when one steps beyond that coil, say out into a wild landscape such as that "land of little rain" which Austin had experienced, one may be revived.[9] It had worked for her, and it was her faith. Inevitably, perhaps, it became her prophecy: in the American Southwest, the land, operating as she said "below all other types of adjustive experience," will pull man by the threads of kinship and inspire him to create a new, earth-harmonious culture. This new way will be, she said, "the *next* great and fructifying world culture."[10]

John Charles Van Dyke appears to have walked, so to speak, some of the same trails as Mary Austin. He does not describe his own transcendent moments in *The Desert* (1904), but the vividness of his writing, and the passion with which he argues against dualism, clearly indicate a post-frontier attitude.[11] Van Dyke made some remarkable solo journeys in Southwestern deserts, not only enduring hardship and ill health, but becoming able to look past or through these obstacles. He seemed to see nature without anthropocentric reference points:

Nature neither rejoices in the life nor sorrows in the death. She is neither good nor evil; she is only a great law of change that passeth understanding [page 129].

The fault is not in the subject [desert wildlife, such as Gila Monsters]. It is not vulgar or ugly. The trouble is that we perhaps have not the proper angle of vision. If we understand all, we should admire all [page 143].

If we could but rid ourselves of the false ideas, which, taken *en masse,* are called education, we should know that there is nothing ugly under the sun, save that which comes from human distortion [page 192].

Van Dyke did not make prophecies, but he did make some strong, affirmative critiques, as in speaking out against reclamation:

The deserts should never be reclaimed. They are the breathing-spaces of the west and should be preserved forever [page 59].

Experience in the Southwest was also decisive in the evolution of Aldo Leopold's thought. Over the course of almost four decades in natural resource management and teaching, Leopold became a significant ethical philosopher, enlarging the logical range of man's concern from just himself and his own kind to the biotic community at large. He had come to the West in 1909 as a forest ranger, and spent the following fifteen years in Arizona and New Mexico. By 1924, having seen the rapacity that marked the sundown years of the frontier era, he was sponsoring wilderness protection in New Mexico. By the 1940's, writing his classic *A Sand County Almanac*, Leopold had developed a comprehensive theory of wilderness as the matrix of civilization:

Ability to see the cultural value of wilderness boils down . . . to a question of intellectual humility. The shallow-minded modern who has lost his rootage in the land assumes that he has already discovered what is important; it is such who prate of empires, political or economic, that will last a thousand years.[12]

There is evidence that Leopold's own intellectual humility along this line traced back to an incident in Arizona, when he took part in the killing of a wolf. In those early days, it was considered politic for forest rangers to cultivate cattlemen by helping eliminate predators. So Leopold, who "was young then, and full of trigger-itch," as he says, was among those who shot a wolf and her pup one day. Making his way down to the bottom of the ravine where the wolves were, Leopold "reached the old wolf in time to watch a fierce green fire dying in her eyes. I realized then," he wrote, "and have known ever since, that was something new to me in those eyes—something known only to her and to the mountain [page 130]." Leopold does not further delineate the experience and its upshot, but in context—the context of denuded mountains and the life gone out of the wilderness—it is clear that he saw in those eyes the light of kinship, the life quality, the unity which held the wolf and the mountain and could have—should have, he thought later—held him too. From this point on, it became personally and ethically important for Leopold to, as his famous phrase has it, "think like a mountain."

Something very like this great change may be seen in the philosophical arc that Joseph Wood Krutch traveled, from 1929 until his death in 1970. In 1929, as we have seen, Krutch expressed in final terms an urban, sophisticated, dualistic pessimism. It seemed to him that "Humanism" and "Nature" were "fundamentally antithetical."[13] A few years later, in a series of essays for the *The Nation* magazine, under the title, "Was Europe a Success?" Krutch concluded that indeed it had been, and he mentioned European philosophy in particular as one of its greatest accomplishments.[14] By the middle 1930's, then, Krutch seemed to have arrived at a paradox: his culture was, he seemed to say, the best that man had attained to, but it appeared nevertheless (as he portrayed it in *The Modern Temper*) to have reached a philosophical wall. At the end of its long, progressive course lay only a knowing, urban alienation.

Krutch's intellectual life for the next forty years can be described as a recovery from that impasse, a slowly accelerating turn toward an affirmation of holism. In this turn, by Krutch's own description and by the evidence of his writings, it seems clear that the Southwest, in particular wilderness in the Southwest, played a crucial role. As early as 1937, as he later described the event in his autobiography, he had "felt a sudden lifting of the heart" while driving across the desert; a sabbatical year in the Southwest, on leave from Columbia University in 1950, seems to have reinforced that earlier experience, for after satisfying the usual post-sabbatical requirement, he moved with eagerness to Arizona.[15]

In his first book from his new life, *The Desert Year*, Krutch already demonstrated strong feelings of empathy with desert wildlife, arguing against mechanistic interpretations:

Let us not say that this animal or even this plant has 'become adapted' to desert conditions. Let us say rather that they have all shown courage and ingenuity in making the best of the world as they found it. And let us remember that if to use such terms in connection with them is a fallacy then it can be only somewhat less a fallacy to use the same terms in connection with ourselves.[16]

This challenge to the old orthodoxy represents a significant softening of Krutch's earlier position. But he went further. In his next book, *The Voice of the Desert*, he turned the challenge inward, onto the workings of consciousness. Now we are not talking merely about opinion and view, but how they originate. Apparently, as Krutch learned more and more about mutualisms in nature, he began to notice changes in his own perception, or heretofore unnoticed levels in it, that were allowing these recognitions of interconnection. He began to question the traditional dualism of the so-called "objective" frame of mind; it did not seem to fit the ecological world he was learning.

Perhaps the mind is not merely a blank slate upon which anything may be written. Perhaps it reaches out spontaneously toward what can nourish either intelligence or imagination. Perhaps it is part of nature and, without being taught, shares nature's intentions.[17]

Krutch explicitly set aside personal mysticism ("I have never practiced the swami's technique for 'heightening consciousness' and I doubt that I ever shall"), but he repeatedly affirmed a nondual interpretation of life and consciousness—in the terms I am using here, a post-frontier view.[18] In *The Great Chain of Life,* 1956, he made the significant argument that as part and parcel of the continuum of all nature, man can share the joy of animals, as in the joyful singing of birds as Krutch heard them, and in such sharing overcome to some degree the alienation that colors our time.[19]

In 1958, Krutch began taking long trips to Baja, California, and the contrast he found between the wildness of a then little-visited land and the furious development of Arizona seemed to make man's modern situation clear to him in a new way. As he reflected more and more on the shrinking wilderness, he began to see in it the pattern that connects and also instructs—or *could* instruct. Apparently, the alienated state that he had described in *The Modern Temper* no longer seemed to him a structural given. Perhaps we can learn our way through it. In one of his last essays for *The American Scholar,* an essay that can be seen as the fruit of nearly twenty years in the Southwest, Krutch asserted that the ecological nature of nature has a spiritual dimension. It has restorative power.

Faith in wildness or in nature as a creative force, has the deeper, possibly the deepest, significance for our future. It is a philosophy, a faith; it is even, if you like, a religion. It puts our ultimate trust, not in human intelligence, but in whatever it is that created human intelligence and is, in the long run, more likely than we to solve our problems.[20]

There are other examples of Southwestern post-frontier consciousness: George Wharton James should not be ignored among turn-of-the century writers, for underneath his tendency toward boosterism there is an experience of the desert given in more personal and profound terms. Among Texas writers, Roy Bedichek and John Graves are, it seems to me, within this tradition—or anti-tradition. And, despite his protestations of redneck realism, Edward Abbey has written some searching reflections on the meeting of mind and nature, particularly in *Desert Solitaire*.[21] I am aware that he has described that book as *"Desert Solipsism,"* but the passion in Abbey is evidence that he is more than just academically dissatisfied with the frontier mind. He is urging us toward something entirely different.

In lieu of enlarging upon these further examples, I would like to speculate on just why this distinctive and to me recognizably consistent pattern has arisen. At first it seems that the phenomenon might be explained in strictly historical terms. Late in the nineteenth century, at the end of the open road, came a moment (when the Pacific Coast had been reached, and the continent pretty much filled in) when further movement seemed temporarily balked. Was there a "window" here, a moment when a frontier-minded population had a chance to look around, and even look at itself? It had been a particularly frenzied century, this fourth and last one of the great European expansion. Toward the end of it, we in America had perhaps begun to see that the dreams of Crevecoeur and Jefferson were not in fact going to be realized. The country had gone in a different direction. We had, as Frederick Turner points out in his excellent study of John Muir, plundered the land mercilessly, and were not discernibly better people for it.[22] Ever since the Civil War had marked the victory of large-scale industrialism, there had been philosophical disquiet, a growing recognition, as exemplified in Walt Whitman's *Democratic Vistas*, of an American "hollowness at heart." The last decades of the nineteenth century, perhaps especially the years around the official (U.S. Census-declared) closing of the frontier in 1890, were for some a time of self-awareness and self-analysis, reform, and social criticism. Stephen Crane, Hamlin Garland, Theodore Dreiser, and John Muir, to take just a few examples, are perhaps prototypal.

So we might simply say that in this intellectual climate, at just the right time, a number of sensitive people happened to enter the most dramatic, eye-opening landscape in North America, a landscape still, then, relatively unspoiled. It also happened to be that part of the country where the most nearly intact Native American cultures still could provide examples. This was, of course, of great importance to writers like Mary Austin, D. H. Lawrence, John Collier, and Frank Waters: they saw in the Indians a wholly different kind of vitality, a centeredness perhaps long lost to a frontier-seeking people.

We could ascribe the post-frontier mind, then, mainly to the seriousness that is said to come to cultures in decline. Another way to look at the phenomenon is to take Mary Austin's view, that the land itself is contributive. One may not have to be a mystic or prophet to support this. Gregory Bateson, for example, in *Steps To An Ecology of Mind*, 1975, and *Mind and Nature*, 1979, makes a scientific argument for the co-dependence of what mainstream Western philosophy has called "subject" and "object."[23] Paul Shepard has also made a scholarly case, in *Nature and Madness*, 1982, for the positive and crucial role that wild places and wild animals play in the growth of a sane outlook.[24] The old model of consciousness as somehow a strictly human possession, an entity, and with it the old model of an exterior world made up of so much neutral stuff, may be breaking down. The intellectual groundwork for seeing life and the world not as Locke or Newton did, but more like Einstein or Heisenberg, seems to have been done. If there genuinely is a major change underway, across the board in human affairs, as Fritjof Capra says in *The Turning Point*, we can say that the old truism about artists may be true once again: the important nature writers of the Southwest seem to have gone on ahead.[25]

ENDNOTES

[1] Joseph Wood Krutch, *The Modern Temper* (New York: Harcourt, Brace, 1929), p. 249.

[2] Sigmund Freud, *Civilization and Its Discontents* (New York: W.W. Norton, 1962), p. 24.

[3] Lewis Thomas, *Lives of a Cell* (New York: Bantam Books, 1975), p. 1. Kenneth Boulding, "The Economics of the Coming Spaceship Earth," in *Global Ecology*, ed. John P. Holdren and Paul R. Ehrlich (New York: Harcourt Brace Jovanovich, 1971), pp. 180-187.

[4] John Muir, *The Mountains of California* (1894; rpt. Garden City, New York: Doubleday, 1961), p. 52.

[5] Clarence Dutton, *Tertiary History of the Grand Canyon District* (Washington: Government Printing Office, 1881), p. 90. Further page references are from this text.

[6] Mary Austin, *The Land of Journeys' Ending* (1924; rpt. Tucson: University of Arizona Press, 1983), p. 40.

[7] Mary Austin, *Experiences Facing Death* (London: Rider and Co., 1931), pp. 239-240.

[8] Mary Austin, *Everyman's Genius* (Indianapolis: Bobbs-Merrill, 1925).

[9] Mary Austin, *A Woman of Genius* (New York: Doubleday, Page, 1912).

[10] Austin, *Journeys' Ending*, pp. 441-42.

[11] John Charles Van Dyke, *The Desert* (1904; rpt., Layton, Utah: Peregrine Smith, 1980). Further page references are from the 1904 edition.

[12] Aldo Leopold, *A Sand County Almanac* (New York: Oxford Press, 1949), p. 200. Further page references are from this edition.

[13]Krutch, *The Modern Temper*, p. 249.

[14]Joseph Wood Krutch, *More Lives Than One* (New York: William Sloane, 1962), p. 241.

[15]Krutch, *More Lives Than One*, p. 308.

[16]Joseph Wood Krutch, *The Desert Year* (New York: William Sloane, 1952), pp. 28-29.

[17]Joseph Wood Krutch, *The Voice of the Desert* (New York: William Sloane, 1954), p. 218.

[18]Krutch, *The Desert Year*, p. 381.

[19]Joseph Wood Krutch, *The Great Chain of Life* (Boston: Houghton Mifflin, 1956).

[20]Joseph Wood Krutch, "If You Don't

Mind My Saying So," *The American Scholar*, 39 (Spring 1970), p. 204.

[21]Edward Abbey, *Desert Solitaire* (New York: McGraw-Hill, 1968).

[22]Frederick Turner, *Rediscovering America: John Muir in His Time and Ours* (New York: Viking, 1985).

[23]Gregory Bateson, *Steps to an Ecology of Mind* (New York: Ballantine, 1975); *Mind and Nature* (New York: Dutton, 1979).

[24]Paul Shepard, *Nature and Madness* (San Francisco: Sierra Club, 1982).

[25]Fritjof Capra, *The Turning Point* (New York: Simon and Schuster, 1982).

BIBLIOGRAPHY

Abbey Edward, *Desert Solitaire*. New York: McGraw-Hill, 1968.

Austin, Mary. *Everyman's Genius*. Indianapolis: Bobbs-Merrill, 1925.

———. *Experiences Facing Death*. London: Rider & Co., 1931.

———. *The Land of Journeys' Ending*. Tucson: University of Arizona Press, 1983.

———. *A Woman of Genius*. New York: Doubleday, Page, 1912.

Bateson, Gregory. *Mind and Nature*. New York: Dutton, 1975.

———. *Steps To An Ecology of Mind*. New York: Ballantine, 1975.

Boulding, Kenneth. "The Economics of the Coming Spaceship Earth," in John P. Holdren and Paul R. Ehrlich, eds., *Global Ecology*. New York: Harcourt Brace Jovanovich, 1971, pp. 180-187.

Capra, Fritjof. *The Turning Point*. New York: Simon & Schuster, 1982.

Dutton, Clarence. *Tertiary History of the Grand Canyon District*. Washington: Government Printing Office, 1982.

Freud, Sigmund. *Civilization and Its Discontents*. New York: Norton, 1962.

Krutch, Joseph Wood. *The Desert Year*, New York: William Sloane, 1952.

———. *The Great Chain of Life*. Boston: Houghton Mifflin, 1956.

———. "If You Don't Mind My Saying So," *The American Scholar*, 39 (Spring, 1970).

———. *The Modern Temper*. New York: Harcourt, Brace, 1929.

———. *More Lives Than One*. New York: William Sloane, 1962.

———. *The Voice of the Desert*. New York: William Sloane, 1954.

Leopold, Aldo. *A Sand County Almanac*. New York: Oxford University Press, 1949.

Muir, John. *The Mountains of California*. Garden City, NY: Doubleday, 1961.

Shepard, Paul. *Nature and Madness*. San Francisco: Sierra Club, 1982.

Thomas, Lewis. *Lives of a Cell*. New York: Bantam Books, 1975.

Turner, Frederick. *Rediscovering America: John Muir In His Time and Ours*. New York: Viking, 1985.

Van Dyke, John Charles. *The Desert*. New York: Charles Scribner's Sons, 1904.

CHARLES BOWDEN

USELESS DESERTS & OTHER GOALS

Let me ask you one question, "Is your money that good?"

—B. Dylan

Any discussion of the natural world and my toils in the wilds must be prefaced by two facts.

I have never been able to read *Walden*.

I like to walk.

Somehow I have wound up scribbling a lot of things about weeds, bugs, beasts, and badlands. Since I can't use the common excuse for such behavior—claiming that Henry David Thoreau made me do it—I will do the next best thing and blame my feet. And all this walking—I am capable of 200-mile stomps through hot, dreary wastelands—has led me to two conclusions which I would like to add to the onward march of Western Civilization: we need more useless deserts and fewer books celebrating the aesthetic glories of Nature.

But, before we explore these two major contributions I hope to add to the intellectual wealth of the republic, I'd like to examine for a moment this hiking frenzy of mine. As a walker I am a disgrace to all the canons of woodcraft, survival skills and aesthetics. I seldom hit the trail without an extra barrel of purple ink in my backpack and my pack itself is a public scandal—grossly stuffed, distended and bloated with

131

the flatulence of my filthy rich and seductive society. I am the person widely mocked, a fool on the trail with 100 pounds of lightweight gear on my back, trudging along with a demented gaze as I eagerly talk to God or a stone. I generally return with blistered feet and a message of oceanic bliss culled from thrilling adventures with cacti and fierce ants.

In my everyday life, I tend to work hard and zealously pursue bad habits. In God's good time, I always go off the rails.

And then I walk.

I think I started walking because of my father—wouldn't be much of a modern American if I passed up a chance to take a shot at dear old Dad—and he was an awesome warrior with his feet. When I was a kid in Chicago I noticed many things: Democrats always won elections, the Cubs always lost baseball games, and every month or so my father would wrestle with some problem that even a cold quart of Blatz couldn't solve. And then he would walk maybe ten, twenty, thirty miles, walk through the Southside, walk through Chinatown, walk through the thieves' market of Maxwell Street, walk to the Loop and beyond. For this work he preferred Army surplus sneakers (with the sides cunningly cut out by his pocket knife so his feet could savor the cleansing city air), old slacks and a stride that would leave a drill sergeant in the dust.

To my father's credit, he never felt the need to utter one word about this walking business. Or about the Nature business. Or the Outdoors business, Environmental business, Conservation business. He was an old-line American who took his whiskey neat and his trees and meadows in total silence. So, while I think I can lay some of the blame for this walking madness on his terrible example, I must stand alone in this matter of blathering about wilderness, ecology, God in the sunset and the urgent need to blow up Glen Canyon Dam.

There is a whole literature about this Nature business and one of the problems I have with this numbing sea of books is that I am almost as unfamiliar with the texts as is the Chamber of Commerce. I would rather stomp through wild ground than read about it. Since I am grossly ignorant about the environmental literature of the Southwest, I think I am well equipped to give you a mercifully short course concerning its outlines and content.

Here is my cheat sheet, should anyone ever quiz you on the significant books about the parched ground of this region. At the turn of the century, John Van Dyke wrote *The Desert* and explained to us that it was bad form to describe as Godforsaken every place that fails to look like Iowa. He saw the desert as a positive landscape rich with aesthetic values and for decades a veritable torrent of similar books,

Charles Bowden has written much about life in the Southwest. He lives in Tucson where he is editor of City Magazine.

poems and paintings have rained down upon the thirsty Southwest and all these works diligently lecture us to appreciate colors in the rocks, the power of the sunsets and to regret that we were not born Hopis. Eventually, this little cottage industry came to center in Santa Fe and Taos. And anyone who would like to feel insensitive, crude and loutish is encouraged to dip into this literature and be properly flogged by the rarified souls who created it.

About the same time in the early twentieth century, a second literature emerged in the region, one forged by conservationists and hunters—in those days these viewpoints were commonly housed in one human body. We have Aldo Leopold arriving in 1909 and spending the next decade busily shooting wolves, bears, deer, birds—just about anything that was foolish enough to wander before his musket. Out of this carnage came one of the truly great American books, *A Sand County Almanac*, a work finished just before his death in the late 1940's. The emotional core of this volume is the Southwest. Leopold taught me two important ideas. Namely, that wild ground can only be saved by people who actually use and live on the ground and that if there is no wild ground we will all go crazy. In keeping with my policy of never reading environmental books, I avoided Leopold until my late 30's. And this particular negligence constitutes one of the major regrets of my life.

A second shooter, much less well known, is Charles Sheldon—responsible in part for the creation of Mount McKinley National Park, among other achievements. Sheldon was the kind of man all honest Americans would like to emulate: by his mid 30's he had made a fortune as a mining engineer, quit work and for the rest of his life did as he damn well pleased. What pleased him was shooting things and he has left us vivid accounts of shooting the Southwestern grizzly (now almost certainly extinct), of blasting the desert bighorn (now reduced to a few mountain peaks where the condominiums have not yet arrived), and of hunting with wild Seri Indians (now properly housebroken and assigned the task of carving endless ironwood curios).

It is very easy, particularly for those of us who feed on John Muir and denounce any killing save of a fat juicy Black Angus, to sneer at people like Sheldon and gaze down upon him and his ilk as primitive and disreputable forebears. Recently, his Southwestern journals (*The Wilderness of Desert Bighorns & Seri Indians*) were privately printed because no academic press was eager to touch such a blood-soaked volume. I happened to buy and read the book and I am here to tell you it is a very good book. Sheldon knew intimately two desert regions I happen to walk a lot—the volcanic Pinacate of Sonora and the Cabeza

Prieta National Wildlife Refuge of Arizona—and his eye for detail and sense of the land made me realize how much a good hunter must become one with the world of his prey. But more importantly, because of nimrods like Leopold, Sheldon, Theodore Roosevelt and others, the Southwest is studded with huge tracts of wilderness set aside to preserve threatened species. Places like the Cabeza Prieta, the Kofa, the Kaibab and many others would not be there for me to enjoy except for the work of these hunters. One of the things you have to consider when you talk about the "environment" and "environmental literature" is that the people who are almost totally absent from audiences such as this—the hunters, those crazed killers with the guns who like to drink strong waters and wear bright colors—those guys have probably saved more ground than all of us, certainly more ground than I ever will with my tiresome scribbling. I love to hike the Growler Valley, the Pinta Sands, the Tule Desert, the Lechuguilla Desert, the Tulerosas and other parts of the Cabeza Prieta in southern Arizona and these thousands of square miles have been set aside and left fairly pristine in order that several human beings a year can enter and try to take down a desert bighorn. This seems a very small and fair price to pay to save such enormous tracts of land.

Anyway, after Van Dyke, Leopold, Sheldon and many others—at least in my scant readings of the literature—come Edward Abbey and Dave Foreman and all the other rowdies who advise us that if we are going into the wilderness to be sure and pack a monkey wrench in our packs. Being by nature incompetent around machines, I find the destruction of such frustrating piles of metal to be just, soothing and clearly part of the divine plan. But this new literature of the '60's, '70's and '80's offers more than Luddite hijinks. I think it puts forth (and resurrects) some clear, moral ideas. First, it asserts that places should not be preserved simply because they are beautiful to look at and make locations for Western movies and Sierra Club calendars, but more importantly because habitats are key parts of ecosystems and we must salvage these biological treasures and protect them from the insistent monotony of our industrial civilization. Second, we must maintain wild ground for our own sanity (a plea that goes back to the Thoreau I have never gotten around to reading) so that people like myself can trot out there and have mystical experiences mixed with copious libations of mescal.

We must not destroy any more wild ground because if we do, we may kill life itself and naturally that means the movie will end for us also. We must not simply appreciate nature, we must fight to save it.

In direct violation of the United States Uniform Penal Code for humanists and intellectuals, these ideas have actually had consequences in the real world. There really are people out there monkey wrenching the bulldozers, chainsaws, oil exploration rigs and other vermin that infest the West and Southwest. And there really are organizations setting aside ground for reasons other than scenic wonder and human recreation possibilities. The Nature Conservancy, for example, reminds me of the Chicago meat packers in the nineteenth century who raided Europe buying El Grecos. The Nature Conservancy goes around snapping up every choice canyon, bog, snakepit, grassland, wasteland, badland, malpais and briar patch.

So we have come a long way. The Anglo pioneers saw this region as a hell hole—take my word for it, they couldn't stand the place. Then around the turn of the century writers pointed out that the deserts and hard mountains and stone plateaus were really quite nice to look at and had a positive place in human consciousness. The early hunters, at least those who could write without using a crayon, shared not only this aesthetic appreciation but also argued that the biological richness of this region must be saved for future generations. And for decades these two viewpoints were refined, notably in the writings of people like Joseph Wood Krutch.

This brings us down to the present literature which builds on the past but adds new angry voices, voices insisting we must take a broader view than simply saving striking landscapes and that we must consider bolder acts than simply scribbling our love of nature or feeding at the trough of federal humanities grants at periodic conferences such as this one.

Now I think this has led us to a problem and the problem is that we are in love with an elegant solution—simply locking land up and saving it for future needs, kind of like stuffing Krugerrands under our mattresses. Whenever I timidly put forth this idea of locking up vast portions of the Southwest and throwing away the key, I am usually told I am an elitist and of course, like any true-blue American steeped in democratic juices, I am an elitist and so are all of you. I get tired of being told I'm an elitist as if the purpose of this nation were to create a population of interchangeable parts. Also, I am baffled: if I walk off into a roadless area with my hundred-pound backpack stuffed with things no sane person would ever need, I'm an elitist. But if I go to town, plunk down $15 grand for a four-wheel-drive war wagon and then proceed to blitzkrieg the desert, I'm considered a populist.

But getting back to the main point, we can lock areas up and we are doing it. That's what all the hollering is about in the struggle to set land aside as wilderness areas, primitive areas, refuges, National Parks, National Monuments, National Grasslands, Wild Rivers and half a hundred tricky headings. This effort is often cloaked with wads of rhetoric, but within this deadening blob of verbiage it is obvious to even me that it is clearly a holding action to shelter parts of the biosphere until this current fire storm of growth passes. The hope is simply that species, habitats and entire ecosystems might survive and flourish again in some future that is less ferocious.

Another aspect of this same task is the work of my friend Gary Nabhan to save the knowledge of earlier generations about the usefulness of indigenous plants for food, fiber and medicine. Most of these species have been assigned to the biological junkpile by our fast food palates and Gary has bravely gone against this cultural drive and insisted we consider eating unspeakable things. I have personally been poisoned by him with a generous helping of tepary beans—a fierce little taste treat that has been banished from our Wonderbread menus. This noble work of saving seeds and recording agricultural practices long abandoned is cleverly disguised under the name Ethnobotany, perhaps so that the modern agribusiness will not notice such subversive activities are taking place.

Clearly we have come a long way in tutoring ourselves about the desert. We bore each other to death announcing that "the desert is beautiful and fragile." You can hardly get a drink in a saloon if you are foolish enough to call these parts "Godforsaken" and the day cannot be far distant when bulldozers will be decorated with scenic murals (perhaps nice Ansel Adams prints). But we have learned to appreciate the desert on our own terms as sensitive spectators and what we have produced is a literature that we all write for each other. These effusions circulate in a refined little circle and we call them Environmental Literature and we all feel quite good about this enterprise. I certainly do. Every time I dip my quill pen and scratch out another immortal sentence my moral self-righteousness practically flies right off the scale.

The trouble is I don't think these wonderful poems, paintings, photographs, essays, books and precious sketches are reaching other people. I live in this community and I don't think most of my neighbors give a tinker's damn about this literature. A lot of them putter around in the out-of-doors but they view these publications with about the same enthusiasm as they would a sex-change operation. In a sense, the literature and its visual aids have become the official state religion—this piety about the beautiful Southwest—and like most religions it is largely ignored. Most of the people who use the land—hunters, the RV people, the Four Wheelers, the trail bike hordes—don't give this literature a moment's thought. They just figure in our books as the demonic forces of darkness that rip the land, pollute the skies, shoot holes in signs and decorate the ground with indestructible beer cans. We actually should cut them in for a chunk of our royalties since they provide so much of the best action in our scribblings playing the sinister Vandals roaring across the pages.

Alas, they are not so different from ourselves. Like almost everyone in the Southwest, they live in a few grotesque cities and have very little contact with the land. I myself am hardly Daniel Boone, but basically a city person. I have lived amid concrete since I was three and I will probably die within easy reach of a parking meter. I visit the wilds the same way people visit the theater—periodically for short, enjoyable episodes.

Let me sum up this mishmash: we all appreciate the desert; we all write and read statements of this appreciation; we all live in cities and have almost nothing to do with this desert we appreciate. Our hearts are in the right place, but our money and lives are all downtown.

Meanwhile our cities keep booming and blotting out desert; our citizens keep increasing and tearing up the desert; our plans all point to a rapid growth that means there will be less desert, less Southwest and more concrete.

I have a few humble suggestions to make to remedy this impasse.

First, let's abolish Environmental Literature. It is has become a pious bore and is the symptom of a sick society that cranks out books on losing weight, how to tune your Ford and oh, yes, we'll have one on the environment also. If we can only punch through the word "environment" we just might reach the reality: we actually live in the environment. It is not something separate from our city lives except in this literature we cultivate that places the biosphere, the various ecosystems, the very juices of life itself in a tidy little arena that we can pick up for our Sunday stroll in the wilds and leave again on Monday morning when we go to work.

Truly, our cities and our lives have altered, mangled and mutilated the world that greeted our ancestors in this region but, even given this fact, we cannot escape the natural world. Under our safe streets the earth still awaits its return to sunlight. Under our cities, the water tables steadily decline and there will be a day of reckoning. We can build our solid houses that wall off the natural world, but the beasts, bugs, plants, floods, droughts, heat waves and cold waves are still out there and will in time knock our dwelling to the ground. The Southwest is a region full of ghost towns and ruins and it does not take a genius to grasp the message of these monuments to human defeat.

If we are going to be healthy we must abolish Environmental Literature and begin to live consciously in the environment, this ball of dirt surrounded by precious gases that has fueled our odyssey in this place for some billions of years. A major step toward this goal will be to face the cities we now ignore as much as possible and all live in. I happen to find this city, Tucson, an ugly, sprawling mess. And I happen to like this city a lot. Ed Abbey once told me, "Tucson is easy to leave, I've left it six times." I've only left it twice so I still have four bullets in my gun.

I think we must create a literature that talks to people here, people living under roofs, driving rush hour traffic, fretting over bills, swilling beer and whiskey on Friday night. In fact, let's junk the word Literature also, a category best used by our descendants rather than ourselves. Our task is not to write for the ages of the English professors, but to write and think for ourselves. And since we live and will continue to live in big human communities almost stripped of representatives of the natural world, let us face that fact and write it.

I must insist again and again that the Southwest is an urban culture (and has been for a century) and everyone is in the cities, safe behind the moat. Our literature as it nows stands deals largely with little pockets of the pre-settlement world, the tops of mountains, the remaining slabs of free desert, those babbling brooks that sparkle in color photos on our calendars—and we justly esteem and take pleasure from such spots and the images they conjure up. We have created a kind of pornography that fantasizes a natural world that barely exists any longer and that we do not live in. And this is dangerous for us and dangerous for the tiny islands of wild ground that survive.

I suspect it is time for me to get around to the title of this talk, "Useless Deserts And Other Goals." I certainly must have touched on "Other Goals" in all my babbling, so I'll now turn to that noble subject, "Useless Deserts." Clearly, I want to integrate human beings into this landscape because I think only then will we have a prayer of saving this region. But I do not think we can economically do this now. There are too many of us, far too many of us for considering the harvesting of wild plants and putting every family on 40 acres with a mule. In this state, there are now 3 million human beings and there is no way that this region can sustain the fuel, fiber and food needs of such a number.

There is little choice but to lock up much of the region if there is going to be any region at all. And by lock up, I mean get rid of the cattle, ban vehicles, ban everything but periodic visits by people on foot.

Here is what we must do. Consider our cities as they now stand as Sacrifice Areas and mandate that future population, if it must come, settle in these places. Set aside certain areas for RV use, for lunatics on trail bikes and other machine-addicted souls and let them tear up the land solely in these zones. We cannot police the entire Southwest, but we can buy off some human appetites by providing areas for their exercise.

Also, we must gather every tidbit of ethnographic lore that we can—I want every old person in North America interviewed and all of Grandma's knowledge about healing herbs recorded. We must stockpile information against the day when our numbers will permit some kind of useful return to the land.

And we must write books explaining all these matters, books that integrate the wild ground and paved ground as much as possible. Books that face the city so that we can at least build some contact between the way we actually live and the way we would like to live.

Such a world would esteem "Useless Deserts," would dread turning its economic might on the wild ground because it would know such ground would vanish at the touch. If the future Southwest turns out to merely replicate the current East and Midwest, then we have no future and neither do the more settled parts of our country. I want books that are written downtown and written around campfires, that sip teas from Sierra cups and that throw down shots in the beer halls. Only if we face what we are—not who THEY are but what WE are—can we have a prayer of not becoming what we all should dread: refined souls who appreciate Nature, heck even buy books about it, but do little beyond witness the final death throes of this hard, free ground.

No more books for people already converted to Nature Worship. No more conferences for people already converted to Nature Worship.

Useless deserts. Useless, useless deserts. Yes.

SELECTED READINGS

Abbey, Edward. *The Monkey Wrench Gang*. New York: J.B. Lippincott, 1975. This book about destroying the noxious dams, power plants, high lines and bulldozers that mar the region has had a life of its own. Largely scorned by critics and never a best seller, it has won an audience and never gone out of print. I know a lawyer in a big legal firm that lives in a three-piece suit and has read it five times. Lenny Bruce once argued that marijuana would be legalized because all the law students were smoking it. Perhaps this novel is planting even more potent seeds.

Austin, Mary. *The Land of Little Rain.* New York: Gordon Press, 1903. Reprint by University of New Mexico Press, 1974. A bedrock piece of the consciousness of the Southwest. This little book will make clear to anyone why this region is different from all the others.

Kesey, Ken. *Sometimes a Great Notion.* New York: Bantam, 1976. Reprint by Penguin, 1977. This is probably the most underrated American novel written since World War II. The tale delivers the basic contradiction of the American West: a population that embodies the most attractive attributes of the republic (aggressiveness, independence, and a lust for freedom) that by acting out these appetites destroys the land which nurtured such behavior in the first place.

Foreman, Dave, ed. *Ecodefense: A Field Guide to Monekywrenching.* Tucson: A New Ludd Book, 1985. This fit-in-your-backpack guide clearly instructs how to destroy bulldozers, traps, power lines, billboards, etc. This volume has been almost totally ignored by the press but its earnest readers pop up from time to time throughout the West.

Hastings, James R. and Raymond Turner. *The Changing Mile.* Tucson: University of Arizona Press, 1965. A text that is rich with then-and-now photographs of the Southwest and which demonstrates the radical deterioration in the region in the century since American settlement. While the book does not present all the answers, it does ask all the key questions.

Leopold, Aldo. *A Sand County Almanac.* New York: Oxford Press, 1949. Reprint by Oxford Press, 1966 and Tamarack Press, 1977. If you are chilled by words like ecology, ecosystem, biosphere et al., read this book and learn what they really mean without having to fuss with jargon.

Mumford, Lewis. *The City in History: Its Origins, Its Transformations, and Its Prospects.* New York: Harcourt, Brace & World, 1961. A grand examination of human efforts to create high density communities. Mumford is always difficult, always cantankerous and always worth the effort. The first 150 pages of this book are loaded with speculations that cannot help but intrigue any resident of the new Sunbelt boom towns that dot the West. Mumford's perspective will cause unease to both technocrat and nature worshipper alike.

Nabhan, Gary Paul. *Gathering the Desert.* Tucson: The University of Arizona Press, 1985. Illustrated by Paul Mirocha; bibliographic essay. A guide to understanding pre-agribusiness agricultural practices and harvests in the Southwest. This book is part of a new budding literature in ethnobotany that searches the ways of the past in the hope of finding some solution for the region's future. In short, the text brings a technical botanical investigation down to street level. Consider also, Richard S. Felger and Mary Beck Moser, *People of the Sea and Desert: Ethnobotany of the Seri Indians,* University of Arizona Press, 1985; L.S.M. Curtin, *By the Prophet of the Earth: Ethnobotany of the Pima,* University of Arizona Press, 1984; and Nabhan's earlier work, *The Desert Smells Like Rain: A Naturalist in Papago Indian Country,* North Point Press, San Francisco, 1982.

Powell, Lawrence Clark. *Southwest Classics: The Creative Literature of the Arid Land.* Los Angeles: Ward Ritchie Press, 1974. The clearest, best and most comprehensive survey of the Southwest's consequence on writers and their works. Literally a lifetime's reading served up in plain English.

Sheldon, Charles. *The Wilderness of Desert Bighorns & Seri Indians.* Phoenix: The Arizona Desert Bighorn Sheep Society, Inc., 1979. An unpretentious, exciting and deadly accurate account of hunting and experiencing the desert Southwest in the early decades of this century. Sheldon's journal entries deliver the land and spare the reader the customary bathos.

Turner, Frederick. *Beyond Geography: The Spirit of Western Civilization Against the Wilderness.* New York: Viking Press, 1980. This is the kind of book your mother always warned you about. Turner makes a quick swing through 5,000 years of human history to discover why the civilizations that came to the Western hemisphere from Europe detested the wild ground they discovered and the people who inhabited that ground. Radical is an overworked word, but in this case it is the right word. The text goes to the root of the matter and no one who reads it will be able to see the world quite the same way as before. Disturbing, exciting and rich in ideas. Do not leave home without this book—sometimes Mom is wrong.

Underhill, Ruth. *Social Organization of the Papago Indians.* New York: Columbia University Press, 1939. The life of a tribe that really did live with and in the desert is clearly presented. Underhill explains what effect such a life had on the ideas and dreams of such a people.

Van Dyke, John. *The Desert.* New York: Charles Scribner's Sons, 1901. Reprint by Peregrine Smith, 1980. A book I find hard to read but which demands our attention because it is the pioneer effort in converting the deserts from badlands to wonderlands.

West, Mae. *Goodness Had Nothing to Do With It.* New York: Woodhill, 1976. I would be less than honest if I failed to mention this volume since it (along with Errol Flynn's *My Wicked, Wicked Ways*) constituted my sole campfire reading when I first learned the desert Southwest during my adolescent hunting days. Few books offer more ample views of Nature and Nature's Way.

Worster, Donald. *Rivers of Empire: Water, Aridity and the Growth of the American West.* New York: Pantheon, 1985. A survey (by a prize-winning historian) of development in the American West that argues the effort to create a technological, hydraulic civilization has been an economic, intellectual, ecological and moral failure and has created a centralized power in direct conflict with the professed democratic aspirations of the inhabitants. The notes alone are worth the price of the book and the survey of earlier theorists (Karl Wiltfogel, Karl Marx, Lewis Mumford et al.) a step in the right direction. Finally, the debate moves beyond the claims of federal bureaucrats and the counter-claims of environmental foes.

ANN ZWINGER

WRITERS OF THE
PURPLE FIGWORT

Being a nature writer and living in the Southwest were not a part of
my life plan. If anyone had asked me twenty years ago if I would ever
write a book, doubtless I would have found the thought too ridiculous
to deserve comment, let alone writing about the natural world. I do not
have fond memories of growing up in the out-of-doors. I loathed camp.
The only fond memories I have of the out-of-doors are of fireflies
floating and blinking on the Indiana summer evening. Perhaps that's
enough.

I am a Johnny-come-lately to both nature writing and the
Southwest. I am aware of my alien status and do not intend to apply
for citizenship for at least another millenium. But I will apply because
I can imagine living nowhere else or doing anything else with my life.
Newcomer that I am, I still find myself stopped dead in my tracks if I
am characterized as a Southwestern nature writer. Where is this
"Southwest," if it exists at all outside our minds? And what is "a nature
writer," if that is indeed what I am?

There's some good hard evidence that the Southwest exists and the
easiest way to define it is in terms of geography. Go pull out your ten-
year-old road atlas as I did, and there it is, neatly bordered by green lines
and type too small to navigate by. The Southwest was, until recently,
a much lesser known part of the country than the settled West Coast or
the over-settled East Coast, or the quiet places in between where I grew
up. Ironically, New England must once have been to London what the

Southwest is to New England—an exotic place so far away that you couldn't go visit it. And when you can't see for yourself, it is easy to create a vision unfettered by reality.

I think that is what's happened to both the "West" and the "Southwest." We've been created out of whole cloth by a world that has no trouble inventing facts. Some years ago I saw an elegant display in Tiffany's window in New York. It was composed of turquoise and diamonds in fabulous array. This was also about the time of "The Santa Fe Look" in clothes, and when *Gourmet* had discovered chile peppers and was printing its first article about Southwestern cuisine. Looking at the Tiffany window, I realized that the Southwest "had arrived." And that the Eastern perception of what the Southwest is was vastly different from mine.

My view is more like that of Captain William H. Emory's, written while he was engaged in surveying the boundary between the United States and Mexico. On November 6, 1846, he wrote that he felt a sense of alienation at this strange Southwestern landscape:

Strolling over the hills alone, in pursuit of seed and geological specimens, my thoughts went back to the States, and when I turned from my momentary aberrations, I was struck most forcibly with the fact that not one object in the whole view, animal, vegetable, or mineral, had anything in common with the products of any State in the Union, with the single exception of the cotton wood. . . .

My present perception is also curiously mixed with stumbled-on images I pick up from Easterners who are here for the first time. Like Wendy in *Peter Pan*, every spring for the last few years I have been going as a natural history consultant on a Sportyak trip down the San Juan River. Easterners on a trip react in much the same way, delivering their comments in tones of dismay. "There aren't any trees! The river isn't nice and clear like a river ought to be, it's brown and you can't even see the bottom! And, it's so dry!"

Of course they acclimate quickly, fall in love with the vistas and the big blue, blue sky and the stars unblurred by city lights, real honest-to-God fresh air, the virtues of beer for restoring the electrolyte balance, and all that marvelous glorious light. Many of them come back. Some stay. Some even become Southwestern writers.

I know why they react that way. I grew up in Indiana, lived in New England, followed my husband to Florida and Arkansas and Kansas, all places of amorphous light. After we moved to Colorado, I frequently

Ann Zwinger has written several natural history books about the Southwest, which she has explored extensively on foot, in boats, and from small airplanes.

returned to Indiana to visit. Indian summers are lovely, lush and thickly green. Falls are exhilarating, full of color and, used to be, the smell of burning leaves, an evocative childhood smell if there ever was one. Springs are redbud and lilacs and soft rains that bless the earth.

But it got so that a couple of days with those obscured backdrops stretched the limit of my disposition. I yearned for the clarity, for the sky that stretched taut blue from horizon to horizon, where the landscape was clearer and closer, where things just made better sense. For me the geographical Southwest is defined by candlepower. A laser beam of a sun. And in my case, there is something addictive about that light.

This addiction to light may not be just unfounded fancy. Until recently it was thought that the tiny pineal gland, of great importance to reptiles in receiving light information, was vestigial in humans, as useless as an appendix. Recent research is suggesting that our pineal gland may directly affect the way we feel about the world, and the lack of light may induce deep depression in many people. Insufficient light may explain why a lot of people get the winter blahs. Exposure to large doses of bright light that contain the full spectrum of natural daylight experienced in wintertime when days are short, has improved the mental health of manic-depressives. A light bulb has been developed, patented, and is now being marketed for this precise therapy.

It is my opinion, unfounded or not, that even the minor flooding of light one gets every day in the Southwest improves one's sense of well-being. The amount and quality of light here makes me—as our local Oldie-Goldie radio station's flagrant grammar describes their music— the light here "makes me feel good." Light gave the Flemish masters those luminous landscapes and the Renaissance painters those pearly vistas; light gave the Dutch painters those billowing skies and the Impressionists their *plein air*. Light gives me a desert and a way of life. This quality and abundance of light cannot help but affect the way one sees the world, literally and figuratively. It cannot help but affect the visual artist, and it cannot help but affect the writer.

Yet when I try to define a Southwestern writer I find it a lot easier to say who isn't than who is. The whole aspect of being a Southwestern writer was summed up in an unexpected way by someone who has nothing to do with Southwestern writing. Jesse Jennings, the dean of Great Basin archaeologists at the University of Utah, writing with an entirely different meaning, titled a 1956 article, "The American Southwest: A Problem in Cultural Isolation."

Lawrence Clark Powell's masterful collection of essays, *Southwest Classics*, gives me a lot of invaluable insight into the widely varied personalities of Southwestern writers. And that probably is the best definition of a Southwestern writer I can come up with, stunning in its simplicity and reassuring in its idiocy: a Southwestern writer is affected by and writes about the Southwest.

But having said that, I'm stumped. I find my confusion symbolized in the concept of the legendary "purple sage" which is neither purple nor sage. When I first moved West I was puzzled by that reference because if "purple sage" meant "sage*brush*" (which I, as a neophyte associated with "the real West"), it was clearly a misnomer. *Artemisia tridentata* has insignificant flowers that bloom in late summer and doesn't fit Zane Grey's image at all.

If "purple sage" meant a member of the mint family, as real sage is, that is to be expected farther north or in shaded montane habitats and not out in the plains and deserts where the deer and the buffalo roam. It was one of the puzzles I never got around to looking up, my theory being that if you hang around a question long enough someone is bound to turn up who will answer it for you.

And sure enough, a couple weeks ago someone just did. I was in the Chihuahuan Desert in Texas when a botanist handed me a stiff branch, filled with silvery leaves and loaded with large lavender flowers. "Here," he said, "is the famous purple sage!" I later saw large patches of it and indeed, it hazes the close horizons with lavender which I could stretch to purple if I chose to be cavalier about colors. But sage it ain't. It's a figwort, the same family to which penstemons and Indian paintbrush belong.

Now that's a fact only a naturalist could love, and that is what I happen to be and the Southwest seems to be a good place to be one. An old-fashioned naturalist to boot, characterized by Jacob Bronowski as "a peculiar Victorian occupation."

I am also a research writer who, like any sane person, prefers research to writing. I admit to days when I positively envy a novelist who is guided by imagination rather than chained by the tyranny of facts. Or the historian with a single-subject focus. Or a geologist. A naturalist has dozens of disciplines with which to deal. My bibliography cards go from the *American Academy of Arts and Sciences* to *Zoology*, my place names from Amargosa to Zzyzx. Perhaps dealing with this amount of heterogeneous material is good for a naturalist. Perhaps it imposes a certain cock-eyed discipline that keeps me from thinking in compartments. It's like picking up pebbles off the beach and rearranging them in ways new to the river, but pleasing to me.

As much as I envy the knowledge and the discipline of the scholars to whom I am so indebted, I am not a scientist reading off computer printouts and chaining together internal events to describe an external organism, or a field geologist endlessly clinking out rocks and building eons. I'm a nutty farflung correspondent on a small part of this planet, in love with what grows and stalks and slithers and trills and calls. Particularly here in the Southwest.

Somewhere in my work day I shall discover that a saguaro can only germinate, sprout and survive beneath a "nurse tree" which it will repay by usurping its patron's water supply. *Plant Physiology* tells me that thorns are leaves that have become so morphologically rearranged that they don't even look like what you think a leaf ought to look like. And even if a leaf looks like what it ought to look like, is it C_3 or C_4 photosynthesis going on inside?

And then I may look up the female glowworm I found in a Utah canyon one night when we were trying to call in a horned owl. Females never get out of the larval stage, and while they are still fat and pudgy and wormlike, mate with winged adult males. Such little curled lights deep in a desert canyon, eternally luminescent and eternally adolescent.

Eternal adolescence. That open-minded enthusiasm which is the bag and baggage of nature writing. In what other profession can you wander a natural world that is so rich that there is always something wonderful just around the bend? In what other occupation is there such joyous reassurance of the ingenuity of living creatures, such marvelous things to be learned, such a continual sense of discovery?

It is that insatiable curiosity that makes me a naturalist-writer, not an environmentalist-writer.

A naturalist is, I suppose, *a priori*, an environmentalist—if by that term you mean someone concerned with the health of the environment. But I think of "an environmentalist writer" as one who writes primarily to change opinion, who has one finger in your shoulder, driving you against the wall, saying, "Look, you slob, what a mess you've made of this earth—NOW what are you going to do about it?"

The environmentalist stance is of necessity an adversary stance. The environmentalist subscribes to a specific vocabulary that contains concise unembellished words directed toward a public audience. The naturalist is less constricted in vocabulary. Words that are rich in imagery and overlaid with meanings, often poetic and evocative, embellish nature writing at its best.

Environmental writing deals in specific knowledge precisely expressed. A lot of environmental writers were literate in the best sense; I think of Jonathan Swift's *A Modest Proposal*. And thank God for Ed Abbey who continues this high sense of irony. The best—and I use that flat word with no qualification—was Rachel Carson.

At worst, environmental writers can be narrow-minded and humorless. When clad in the armor of their own self-righteousness, they can be absolutely insufferable. I give you that phrases like "extinction is forever" are not your basic jolly, but too much doom and gloom has a tendency to alienate and depress, bore, or at worst, cause irreparable rifts. You need only count the number of "If you're hungry and out of work, eat an environmentalist" bumper stickers to know that environmentalists are *not* communicating with a large segment of the public. Miners who mine soft coal in Ohio, construction workers who build dams, may not publish in scholarly journals, but they can be hungry, concerned about job and family, and not convinced by "SAVE THE ENVIRONMENT" posters.

In taking a hard stance, many environmentalists have alienated the very people with whom we need to communicate. Joe Sixpack is not stupid. But he needs to be addressed in ideas that make sense to him, and I'm not sure telling him that his factory is closing and he's losing his job because of environmental restrictions is making any Brownie points for the environment.

I've been brought up short twice in recent years on just this subject. I was driving through the lovely Virginia countryside with a utility engineer. There was an unusually large swatch cut right through the trees and over the crest of an otherwise virgin hillside to accommodate a high tension line. Without thinking, I blurted out, "Oh, why did they have to do *that*?"

The engineer looked at me with disbelief and replied, somewhat soberly, "Oh, that's beautiful—carrying power to people who need it in their daily lives." Gullpp.

The second time was a few months ago when my husband and I drove out to Sand Mountain, a huge flowing dune with beautiful proportions lying east of Fallon, Nevada. We stopped at the foot to gaze upward and deplore the number of dune buggies buzzing like angry wasps all over it. When we started the truck to leave there was a horrible THUNK that said the back wheels were a foot deep in sand. Some of the dune buggy people came to help push us out. Since I have a delicate stomach when it comes to an engine screaming in distress, I stepped out and struck up a conversation with one of the women standing by. She spoke with a crisp English accent and told how captivated she was by this dune field. She said they drove all the way here from California because, "When I get up there on that knife rim," and her arm described a huge sweeping gesture, "it's—it's just breathtaking, it's so beautiful."

Her aesthetics are not mine. Noise spoils my view. But I have to accept the validity of her reaction. She is the person we need to communicate with and the sooner the better. As Reyner Banham has said, the problems aren't problems of the environment as much as they are problems of people getting along with people. Courtesy goes a lot farther in getting a point across than dogmatic confrontation.

The chain of principles upon which I operate are simple—or, if you will, simplistic. If you can entice someone to look at a facet of nature they may get curious. If they get curious they may make an attempt to learn something about what they're seeing. If they learn something, that becomes an irrevocable part of their experience. If it becomes part of your experience you are more likely to appreciate and enjoy it. If you appreciate and enjoy, you're less likely to destroy. It becomes "yours" in the *only* way anything can be owned—in your head. And at the very best, you come to have an understanding of the worth and intricacy of the natural world and man's place in it.

Obviously this is too slow-moving a philosophy for the speed of the modern world and the environmentalist who sees the world going to hell in a handbasket. My only excuse is that I'm comfortable with it, albeit with a freight of guilt. I reassure myself that if there is any occupation in which you've got to be comfortable with yourself, it's writing. You cannot get out there and flag wave if you don't like flags. Or waving.

Part of my guilt problem is that I was brought up in a family that believed that, if there was anything left after getting food on the table and a roof over your head, you contributed to your community—this was not middle-class noblesse oblige, but a deep-seated sense that because you were human you had the capacity to leave the world a little bit better than it was when you came into it, whether it be an improved social condition, a garden to please the eye, or a helping hand to someone who needed it. It was a moral order that I interpret in the broadest sense possible.

So I ask myself: is writing natural history a useful and worthwhile occupation? Am I moving mountains as I might were I an environmentalist? More accurately, am I keeping mountains from being moved?

Can a naturalist be an effective environmentalist simply by being low-key? I think of Rachel Carson. She began as a natural history writer and ended as a flaming environmentalist who brought about massive change. She could not have been the latter without the former. *Silent Spring* is a landmark book. But, I must admit, *The Edge of the Sea* is the most beautiful book she ever wrote and I ever read. It is my ideal of a natural history book.

If this world is to survive in any kind of health, it will be from the combined efforts of naturalists *and* environmentalists because different people respond to different prompts—different oaks for different folks. The low-key approach with which I am comfortable does not not galvanize people like a good healthy panic. It's a cynical fact of life. I just saw the list of things that concern people this year. Last year everyone was up in arms about acid rain. Acid rain was "in." This year it has fallen below "littering," almost last on the list.

I find this the earmark of a trendy approach to the environment. The public responds to external stimuli that may be variously orchestrated, and does not have the long-term devotion to problems that deserve long-term solutions. Much the same point was made at a recent Arid Lands conference in Tucson—that our political leaders are seriously de-coupled from the environment. They are, for the most part, lawyers, political scientists, economists—all disciplines that put their faith in man's ability to manipulate the environment to his own betterment. I don't know whether to laugh or cry at such monumental hubris. We all know that Mother Nature is not above putting two "hundred year floods" on year one-hundred of the first century and year one of the next. People who build in floodplains fool with that lady at their peril. Given that politicians have to get re-elected, their choices made vis-à-vis the environment tend to be splashy and eye-catching, often choices that in the long run may be deleterious to the environment. This bodes ill for the future. We do have some probable solutions. We seem not to have the political means by which to implement them.

I'm not sure that a lot can be done about that, by an environmental writer or a nature writer or an anyone else. Nothing shows me that we profit from history. We seem predisposed to act on the short-term gain, not the long-term necessity. I am forced to conclude that there is a self-destruct chromosome in our genes.

So much for sober mature assessments. Against that dour outlook I also find myself reassured, even joyous, when I deal directly with the natural world itself. It works well in the way that the people world does not. I can positively assure you that the sun will set in the west this afternoon, and rise in the east tomorrow. The sun will not indulge in the *non sequiturs* of modern living like highjacking your airplane or damming a great canyon to produce power for electric toothbrushes in Los Angeles.

The ingenious adaptations of the plant and animal world are cause for celebration. They have met the enemy and co-inhabited. The elasticity in nature is marvelous, as is the opportunism in evolution. This and many other things bode well for the natural world as a whole. As I observe it, the natural world is still working a whole lot better than it should. In its complexity and intricacy it wins some and loses some— but mostly it wins, and sometimes it wins big.

Humans tend to get emotional about nature and jolly up the hard edges with classy phrases like "Extinction is forever." So? Is there such a thing as temporary extinction? I am irrevocably committed to the maintenance of the richness of the species fabric of our world. But our human view of how irrevocable is the loss of a species does not necessarily jibe with nature's view, which has been pretty flagrant about doing away with lumberers and plodders and flappers and sloshers— all those who were fitted to another kind of world than the one in which they found themselves. I suspect that quite possibly one of those extinct species is going to be *Homo sapiens*. What's so bad about that? We had our turn. I have no apologies for being human. There's not much that anyone here can do about it except cheer for the survivors and wish them well.

I write, as I'm sure a great many writers do (and perhaps especially Southwestern writers), for the love of this world. Writing gives me a chance to indulge a ravenous curiosity, to get far away to remote places where I can get my head on straight, deal with blisters on my heel instead of my psyche. I am a born wanderer, full of desultory genes. I regard nature writing, of all the things that I could have fallen into, as the most felicitous.

I have no illusions—I'm one of the "haves" in this world. But is nature writing a luxury for which we no longer have space or time? Am I as outmoded as the crane fly, wafting out its days, the gadfly of the Diptera, replaced in evolution by the super-efficient housefly?

Well, so be it. Let my search be for the holy grail of accuracy. Making a silk purse out of a kangaroo rat's ear. Playing with words, juggling and prodding words. Chucking them under the chin. Sautéing and scrambling and skewering words. Running and jumping and playing tag with words.

I am being flippant, you understand, because what I am talking about is too important to me to be serious about. In case you find me unmotivated and cavalier in my attitude about my avocation, let me relate a dream I had several years ago. Unlike most dreams, it has not faded with time. Whenever I call it to mind it comes back full-blown, answering to all six senses.

I was seated in a glorious meadow with a 360-degree horizon, somewhat like a Southwestern desert grassland in the spring, I suppose. The light lay opalescent on every blade of grass and every petal, delineating each in exquisite detail. I could see beyond boundaries of palisade tissue, beyond barriers of protoplasm, into the very swarming of the cell itself. The world was never more beautiful.

Somewhere, off the edge, off the horizon, there had been a nuclear holocaust. Everyone I loved was gone. I was absolutely alone. Yet— there was no sadness, only a sense of infinite serenity.

In my lap were my familiar yellow notepad and pencil. I had been charged with describing this world because shortly there would be no one left, including me, who could tell of the shades and the shadows, the little breeze just before dawn on a river beach, how the stars tracked from yesterday to tomorrow, how the beetle larva stirred in the bark and the yucca moth laid her eggs, how the hermit crab clowned in a shell too big for it and the pelican rode the cushion of air on the ocean's surface. Only through words could those who came after know how supremely magnificent this natural world was.

Only words could tell of laughter in the sunshine and how it felt to trek the wild places, how it was to smell a mushroom and how cool and heavy it felt in the hand, how it was to taste a wild sun-warmed raspberry just pulled off the bush at noon, how it was to listen to the liquid song of a canyon wren in the evening, how it was to lean against a wall of Navajo sandstone and feel the grainy wind embedded in it, how it was to watch an evening primrose open in the warmth of your cupped hand, and how a silly moon smiled at such foolishness.

No one would know these things if I did not take time out from dying to put it all into words that would remain hanging in the dry desert air, suspended with a life of their own, witnesses to grace and coherence. That was all that mattered.

The words.

BIBLIOGRAPHY

Abbey, Edward. *The Monkey Wrench Gang.* New York: J. B. Lippincott, 1975.
————. *Down the River.* New York: Dutton, 1982.

Banham, Reyner. *Scenes in America Deserta.* Layton, Utah: Peregrine Smith, 1984.

Carson, Rachel. *Silent Spring.* New York:

Fawcett, 1978.

————. *The Edge of the Sea*. Boston: Houghton Mifflin, 1951.

Emory, William H. *Report on the United States and Mexican Boundary Survey, under the Direction of the Secretary of the Interior*. Senate Executive Document 108, 34th Congress, 1st Session. Washington, D.C.: A.O.P. Nicholson, 1857.

Lavender, David. *The Southwest*. New York: Harper & Row, 1980.

Powell, Lawrence Clark. *Southwest Classics: The Creative Literature of the Arid Land—Essays on the Books & Their Writers*. Tucson: University of Arizona Press, 1982.

Swift, Jonathan. "A Modest Proposal for Preventing the Children of the Poor People in Ireland from being a Burden to their Parents or Country; and for making them beneficial to their publick." (Original pamphlet published in 1729; available in many anthologies.)

REYNER BANHAM

HAVING IT ALL:
PARTISAN GREED AND
POSSESSION OF THE DESERT

I am some sort of impostor around here—not a desert expert, but just an enthusiast. I have no philosophy or political program for the future of the Southwest, and the desert remains for me a wild, strange place. I am a city boy, born and bred, and the likes of London and Los Angeles will always be for me good and reassuring places. Unlike the Navajo detective in Tony Hillerman's *The Ghostway*, I don't get lost. The wilderness for me will never be the city; I know where the wilderness is—it's outside there, where the wild animals are, beyond the fly-screens on the hotel windows. I could hear them trying to get in all night!

But I could sense again, behind last night's cheap and comforting laughs about Los Angeles and Phoenix in the panel presentations, the thing that I still find most disturbing about the American Southwest and any thoughts we may have about its future: the barely suppressed paranoia. Last night we seemed politely agreed to call it just "nostalgia for a lost past," but nostalgia—as it is commonly understood—does not have such a high content of resentment, so keen a desire for revenge because "it's got to be somebody's fault." Indeed, this sense of some needling paranoia of loss had come back to me even before I arrived here to speak, because the current issue of *California Magazine* contains an article by my colleague, Page Stegner, on "Mysteries of the Mojave," (November 1985).

155

Now Page Stegner is all right: heavy guy with a pick-up truck, prepared to sleep rough if necessary, and with some robust opinions to match. But Page also has the old Desert Paranoia, the truculent insistence on getting-them-bums-off-a-my-property:

He observes my California plates and asks if I, too, am in Parker for the jet-boat races. I tell him no, I'm just down checking out my desert, seeing if it needs watering or weeding.

"Your desert," he says, "Ha ha ha."

I don't know what's so funny. It is my desert. It's also *his* desert. Over three quarters of the region is federally owned land, some of it (three million acres) in national monuments and state parks, another three million acres in military reservations, and the rest of it (twelve-and-a-half-million acres) Bureau of Land Management territory administered for the American people by the Department of the Interior. . . .

Unfortunately he is an increasingly common type. He has his counterparts in the operators of off-road vehicles . . . who seem to feel that it is their "right" as members of a free society to run their machinery whenever and wherever they damn well please, regardless of the effect on wildlife habitats, fragile soil and plants.

"I don't tell you where to drive your car, do I?" one truculent dune-buggy owner tells me during an inadvertent lunch counter interview I conduct over an Amboy burger in the town of the same name.

"Give me your address," I tell him. "Next time I'm in your town, I'll come drive it on your lawn."

It seems to me that this kind of attitude does not bode well for the future of the desert, or any other parts of the Southwest. It shows a lust for personal possession that seems to me morally queasy as well as legally questionable. The proposition that the public domain is "my" land, just because the "I" is a member of the public, shows a poverty-stricken unawareness of the different degrees of ownership, possession and stewardship that the Anglo-Saxon conception of law can envisage and encompass. The situation of the parcel of desert sand on which the dune-buggyer proposes to drive his machine is very different, in law, from that of the suburban front lawn over which Stegner is just as truculently offering to drive his truck. United States law invests personal property and private real estate with inalienable rights for the owner very different from those public rights that inalienably inhere in Federal and State lands—and I believe that Page Stegner and the very large proportion of the Southwestern population who agree with him, have got it all wrong in adopting that attitude they do (though political

Reyner Banham, architectural historian from Great Britain, teaches at the University of California at Santa Cruz.

realism about the future of the desert Southwest means that this attitude cannot be ignored, since it pervades all constituencies).

Survival means sharing, holding in common, but this is not necessarily a simple matter. The public land of the United States, the "open range" or whatever we like to call it, inherits many characteristics of the common lands of the ancient European tradition. Those lands were held by no one individual, but by everybody in the community, according to some socially accepted rule book, but were worked by each individual for private good. Each individual might then be taxed or tithed for the value of part of the product and subject to some marginal regulation for the maintenance of good husbandry. More importantly, there was an implicit obligation of stewardship, to maintain the land in good heart, or even improve it.

All this, of course, is much more complicated than the simplistic eye-for-an-eye, tooth-for-a-tooth, one-on-one property relationships based on absolute title that are understood to underlie a market economy, and the "me" generation is not the first to have problems in distinguishing between the simplicity of "mine" and the complexities of "ours"—complexities that multiply almost exponentially with the number of interests that constitute the "we."

No one body can call the desert "mine," even though that body may have many members and a nation-wide constituency, and it is in the behavior of such large bodies that much of the trouble starts. The Sierra Club does not own the Mojave, nor does the ranching industry, though both tend to behave as if they did, or expected to in the near future. If the Mojave comes anywhere near belonging to any one body at all, it must be to the Bureau of Land Management, which holds its territory in stewardship for the good of all the rest of us—and has therefore to internalize the complexities and contradictions of this situation.

You see this in the day-to-day operations of the Bureau—and of course it is those daily and local actions that bring out the paranoias of the constituents. The BLM clearly understands its duties to lie in the balancing out of the rival claims of the Page Stegners, the off-roaders, the ranchers, the bird-watchers, the miners and all the other would-be possessors of the public lands. What else could they do? Well, in an ideal universe they might be able to occupy a more morally and ecologically responsible role than that of simply mixing and matching these rival claims. They might be able to take a longer view that genuinely envisages a more humane and constructive future, rather than having to spend every day hoping to get through to five-thirty without disaster.

Notice that I said "rival claims," not "differing needs" or "legitimate desires;" these are matters of practical politics— *Realpolitik*, even—whose rule book requires high bidding, so that paranoid rivalries are re-enforced by Rule Number One: "Ask for a hell of a lot more than you could possibly need, in order to be sure of getting enough to satisfy the greed of your constituents." In practice, in the Southwest that "hell of a lot more" is a precise figure and the same in every case: *Everything*. Never ask for less than the *entire* Mojave, or *all* the water of the Owens Valley or whatever, and be sure to get it now because the Native Americans want the *whole lot* back. The reasons for these totalizing claims are various, ranging from the preservation of the freedom of the individual to the preservation of the entire biosphere, and they are usually justified.

Ecological and environmental lobbies see the preservation of the desert as an holistic affair, from which nothing relevant may be omitted, and they are probably right. Deserts are expansive ecological systems with fuzzy edges and you have to draw a very wide map to get in everything that might matter, while inside the map no blank patches may be left, because you dare not leave anything unaccounted for, and nothing may be handled piecemeal. In other words, if you are going to preserve the desert, preserve the lot or don't bother; exclude every single activity that might crack its delicate crust, from motorcycling to mining. But why stop at activities that begin with the letter M? In some places, the ecosystem is claimed to be so weak that even backpacking could ruin it. Who knows what permanent damage has been done by the relentless poking of triplets of holes in that delicate crust by the legs of the tripods that support surveyors' theodolites, bird-watchers' telescopes and Ansel Adams's camera? Nor what permanent disruption to the climatic system of North America may be caused by the exclusion of sunlight from the increasing acreage of desert crust that is shaded by solar energy installations. There is no known human activity that is absolutely harmless to the desert: some are relatively less harmful than others, that is all.

But neither paranoia nor the normal posturings of adversary politics can operate in morally relative terms; they only operate with absolutes. This is absurd, this absolutism! The whole argument may appear absurd—reasonable people don't operate in this way; they are prepared to draw the line somewhere, as the Bureau of Land Management has to do every day of the week. But wherever you draw the line, somebody will be on the other side of it, screaming that their citizen rights have been denied, their freedom abridged. And not because they are criminals or perverts, but because of the very nature of the Southwest and American perceptions of it.

The desert is, for Southwesterners above all others, both the symbol and the substance of their freedoms. A desert fenced off might just as well not exist, its preservation an exercise in abstract futility if no one can enjoy it. A desert managed in any way at all cannot be enjoyed, even if one has access to it, because it is not the unregulated terrain of the desert myth. And this is the dilemma facing all true desert freaks, including myself. If the only way to preserve the landscape that we love is to fence it off—then don't bother, because it will cease to be the landscape of ultimate personal opportunity and ultimate personal responsibility, the proving ground of the free spirit.

There are two points at issue here—though they seem to become the same point. Firstly, as every desert freak knows, a desert that is managed might just as well be a—Yuk!—National Park, with controlled admission, parking lots and signs telling you what to do and even where to look, and that would be, as every desert freak also knows, just the first step on the downhill path to Disneyland. That is totally unacceptable except that—point two—if you are going to manage the desert at all, you might do very much worse than to hand the whole thing over to Disney Enterprises. Their motivation—profit—is something everybody can understand (unlike some of the motivations of the Park Service, which can be totally inscrutable) and their expertise in managing things is vastly greater; they would remove litter as soon as it was dropped, and they would keep up appearances.

That is the point where the two considerations merge. Only an actively managed ecology, desert or otherwise, will be stable enough to go on looking the same, will go on being the desert we have learned to love. The Untouched-by-Human-Hand approach can be remarkably destructive of Beloved-by-Human-Eyes scenery. One of the greatest shocks of my career as an eco-tourist was to arrive in Yosemite and discover Mirror Lake replaced by a couple of acres of stinking mud, not because of improper human interference, but because the Park Service had inscrutably convinced itself that it was morally improper to interfere with natural processes like the water-flow or the silt build-up in the lake. So, in a dry season there is no lake and when the silt has built up enough, the lake will disappear forever, wet season or dry. The awful truth about the deserts seems to be that they probably *need* human interference in order to remain desert, just as some of them were created by human interference in the first place, like the Moghreb of North Africa, and others around the Mediterranean Basin.

We are in the desert irreversibly, and must accept our responsibility. We must recognize that no single claim, program, power or usage can sustain the desert or deserts, the characteristic ecology of the Southwest, in the form and availability that most of us want. We may have to face the alternatives of complete anarchy or, at best, "Benign Neglect." We all have different deserts and usages in mind anyhow, but the acreage on which these facts and fantasies can be performed is finite. We are going to have to share the available land, and to share on a changing daily-adjusted basis. We are going to have to be nice to people we would rather see dead, compromise some cherished ambitions and values, take responsibility for our own actions, share responsibility for the actions of others, defend the weak against the wicked, and so forth.

If that sounds suspiciously like urban life in New York or Los Angeles or—worse—Phoenix, then let us face it, we are simply talking about the ground rules for a productively civilized life in a real human community. We are not talking about some unspoiled Garden of Eden, and if we were, then we would be the serpents in it, the sly despoilers. To minimize the damage that we can do to one another and our beloved desert, there seem to be only two real alternatives: to resign our responsibilities to some Hobbes' Leviathan, be it the Park Service or some commercial body, that will tell everybody what to do and where to do it. Or to retain our responsibilities and to recognize that while we have rights, we will have to sacrifice some of them. The future of the Southwest as a habitat for Man and Beast, Vegetables and Minerals, seems to depend on our recognition that we are going to have to share it, that we *can't* have it all.

Lawrence Clark Powell, former UCLA University Librarian, is Professor Emeritus at the University of Arizona.

LAWRENCE CLARK POWELL

THE FOUNTAIN AND THE WELL: SOURCES OF SOUTHWESTERN LITERATURE

During sixty years in and out of this old cowtown Tucson—the last fifteen as a taxpaying, voting resident—I have sometimes wondered if there could happen here what happened in Santa Fe in the '20's and '30's. That was when that older Pueblo witnessed an explosion of arts and crafts by artists, writers and publishers of books, periodicals, and a newspaper. The self-appointed leader was the formidable Mary Austin who thought nothing of telling off Mabel Luhan and Willa Cather. Mere men she didn't bother with. Today in Santa Fe only the embers remain of that brilliance. The beautiful people from beyond the Sangre de Cristos have bought the town body if not soul. Except for summer opera, chamber music and a book arts festival, the town is dead.

What has Tucson in common with Santa Fe? The not-to-be bought assets of antiquity, history, geography, and a threefold ethnic fusion. Both towns shine brighter because of their neighbors—Phoenix and Albuquerque: the power centers of their states as well as warnings of reckless growth.

To me the most significant thing about this conference is that it grew from the grass roots of the public library, not from the manicured turf within the walls of the university. During the years of its sponsorship with funding by the National Endowment for the

Humanities, the public library has not neglected the university's resources, as it reached over the wall to co-opt such as Big Jim Griffith, Bunny Fontana, Dave Laird, Paul Carter, Larry Evers, Cecil Robinson, and Gary Nabhan. It even went to Northern Arizona University for the one-of-a-kind Jim Byrkit who wears no man's collar.[1]

We who play our games within the walls know how confining academic life can be if you let it be. Not until an academician fights his way to the top can he afford to relax and be his truest self. By then he has either burned out or become an administrator. Yet we have the example of a local administrator not being sterilized by his job—the one who had something to do with photography while standing off the legislators, yet also found time to illustrate two beautiful ethnological books written by El Conejito, as well as writing a third on the black and white artful science he practices.[2] If the sciences have always been the University of Arizona's claim to fame, the creative arts are coming along fast, providing the artists don't get hungry and leave for a better soup kitchen. Young new leadership and editorship at the University of Arizona Press promise an exciting future for that institution. A university's greatness can be measured by its press as well as by its library.

If the Tucson Public Library can maintain momentum, hang on to its creative staff who sponsor events such as this, and at the same time continue to draw on the university for creative talent, there could occur a cultural explosion like the one in Santa Fe fifty years ago. Already present in the Old Pueblo are the cultural layers of peoples who have dwelled here where water once flowed and is now pumped. A long human presence in this river valley has deposited ages of history, folklore and tradition, all meaningfully presented in the library's first Sonoran Heritage program.[3]

Waiting to flower and fruit is a rich bed of nutrients in which the arts and sciences are nourished. Although we deplore runaway growth, we can also see positive aspects. Growth means wealth, wealth means power—power that can be pre-empted by the crafty and made to serve culture. Needed are a few rich leaders with vision and voice who can persuade their even richer, more powerful fellows to follow and to fund.

In the past couple of generations—and by generation I mean about fifteen years—we have seen this happen in Los Angeles where a Dorothy Chandler and a Franklin Murphy, both of the *Times-Mirror* dynasty, led in the transformation of that sometime Queen of the Cow counties into what today is California's power center, both economic and cultural.

What Tucson lacks is a medium for visionary and eloquent spokesmen. Our two largest local newspapers are both absentee-owned and establishment-oriented, dependent upon advertising for the profits they are taking from the community. As fair as both are in most areas, they give small comparative space to the creative arts. In their financial profits they take more than they give.

What comes first in a cultural flowering, the renaissance itself or those who first recognize what has happened, then proclaim and lead it? Leaders are followers at first until they realize what is happening, then organize and give it voice. The creative are often at first obscure, even invisible. In Tucson those voices will be of the young or middle-aged, not the old.

Whatever Tucson's cultural destiny, if it is to have lasting significance, it must grow from native soil, from the grass roots, and though local in origin, it must be infinitely translatable. Here words of Yeats are pertinent—ones addressed to his countrymen at the time of the Irish Renaissance:

I would have our writers and craftsmen master their history and their legends and fix upon their memory the appearance of mountains and rivers and make it all visible again in their arts, so that Irishmen even though they had gone a thousand miles away, would still be in their own country.

Masterpieces are few and unique. Many elements have to be right: time, place, and person, plus that alchemical element called style, by which something common is transformed into something precious. It is like the combination that opens a bank vault—a cunning thing, not to be attained by a random twirling of the dials. In literature as well, many elements must be brought into conjunction, whereby life is seen through language in perfect register.

How can we anticipate posterity and foresee what it will deem to be Southwestern literary masterpieces? We can't. "Will time say nothing but I told you so?" Auden asks and then answers, "If I could tell you I would let you know."

"A writer's books are tickets in a lottery," Stendhal said, "the drawing for which takes place a hundred years after the writer's death."

In five more years Melville will know which of his books wins the lottery. Yet from the time he wrote *Moby Dick* in 1850, he knew it was that book and not *Typee* that held the winning ticket. "I have written a wicked book," Melville exulted in a letter to Hawthorne, "and feel spotless as the lamb."

So what *do* I mean by the fountain and the well? One writer and two of his books will illustrate what I mean: John Steinbeck and his *The Grapes of Wrath* and *East of Eden*. The first jetted from the fountain, the other was pumped from a deepening well.

I knew Steinbeck up to and through *The Grapes of Wrath*. I was one of the earliest critics to recognize his achievement and potential as revealed in his earliest books. The best novelist since Frank Norris, I called him. I went on to form a complete collection of those first books—*Cup of Gold, Pastures of Heaven, To a God Unknown, Tortilla Flat, Of Mice and Men*, and *In Dubious Battle*—all of them inscribed to me by Steinbeck.

I heard from him by postcards during his field work on *The Grapes of Wrath*, as he followed the crops down state. Once he wrote me with his back against an irrigation ditch next to a squatters' camp. In a spidery hand he could get a thousand words on the back of a government postcard. His early manuscripts were written in the same careful hand in blank ledger books. His father had been the treasurer of Salinas County.

Completing that one masterpiece, as it fountained from him, took a heroic push as he sought to control the flow, his wife Carol revising along behind him. At the same time he was racked by rheumatism contracted in the wet fields and orchards. The effort left him exhausted. I don't think he ever fully recovered.

The more he succeeded, the worse everything got. He ignored Trollope's advice: "Success is a poison to be taken late in life and then only in small doses." The violent reaction to his masterpiece by his native state embittered him. He bought a divorce from his wife with the $100,000 the movies paid for *The Grapes*. He then moved East and entered the long decline which led ironically to the Nobel Prize. The taproot through which his creative stream had risen in a powerful artesian flow had been cut.

His other long book, *East of Eden*, was laboriously pumped from a deepening well. This is evident in the journal he kept while writing the book—a daily journal letter to his editor, Pat Covici. Published posthumously as *Journal of a Novel*, it documents what it cost to pump life into that manuscript. His latest biographer predicts that the journal may outlive the novel.[4]

I am unsure of the value of creative writing courses and workshops, perhaps because I have never taught or been taught in one, although I was told by one critic that my two "Classics" books are as much about the sources and act of writing as about the finished writing itself.[5]

This is not saying that I have never learned anything. I had teachers such as Aldous Huxley, Robinson Jeffers, Henry Miller, and D.H. Lawrence's widow Frieda. Consider Huxley, or the prolific polymath Robert Payne, or whatever you call Henry Miller. As a university librarian, I served their need for books and information, and with them I talked books and writing, especially at day's end when my office at UCLA Library had closed and we could converse without interruption. *Those* were my courses in creative research and its products.

Is there a way out of the drying depths into which Tucson has dug itself? Without voices crying in this urban wilderness now spreading around us, there will be no way out. Lord, give us leaders with vision and voice, ones who proclaim that although this is the way it now is, it need not forever be. Lacking such voices and leaders, followers and funders, we are doomed to dwell in a hole of our own digging.

Euphoric though we now be, our hope does not lie in conferences and committees with which we tend to indulge ourselves. Only in the individual lies our future—in solitaries spinning away in the silence of their own cocoons, toiling while the city plays or sleeps. Cultures rise from the beginnings of a few strong and sure ones. Remember the faraway few great Greeks? Shakespeare's England? Emerson's New England? And nearer our time, Mary's Santa Fe?

Do we have such a future? "If I could tell you I would let you know."

ENDNOTES

[1] James S. Griffith, Director of the Southwest Folklore Center, University of Arizona; Bernard L. Fontana, University of Arizona Field Historian; W. David Laird, University of Arizona Head Librarian and editor of *Books of the Southwest: A Critical Checklist of Current Southwestern Americana*; Paul A. Carter, Department of History; Larry Evers and Cecil Robinson, Department of English; Gary Nabhan, formerly with Office of Arid Lands, currently with Phoenix Botanical Gardens; James Byrkit, Department of Geography, Northern Arizona University, Flagstaff.

[2] "El Conejito" is "Bunny" (Bernard) Fontana, author of *Tarahumara: Where Night is the Day of the Moon* (Flagstaff: Northland Press, 1979), and *Of Earth and Little Rain: The Papago Indians* (Flagstaff: Northland Press, 1981), which were illustrated with the photographs of former University of Arizona President John P. Schaefer, now of Research Corporation in Tucson.

[3] Funded by the National Endowment for the Humanities in 1978, this three-year project introduced the history and culture of Sonoran desert peoples to over 100,000 people who came to the library's programs. It won an Award of Merit from the American Association for State and Local History.

[4] John Steinbeck, *The Grapes of Wrath* (New York: Viking Press 1939); *East of Eden* (New York: Viking Press, 1952); *Journal of a Novel* (New York: Viking Press, 1969).

[5] Lawrence Clark Powell, *California Classics: The Creative Literature of the Golden State* (Los Angeles: Ritchie, 1971); *Southwest Classics: The Creative Literature of the Arid Land* (Los Angeles: Ritchie, 1974).

This book was designed by A. Tracy Row. The type was set in Baskerville and Megaron by A & W Typesetting Company of Tucson, Arizona; the book was printed by Fabe Litho, Ltd., of Tucson; it was bound by Roswell Bookbinding, Phoenix, Arizona.

Use this book as a basic lecture
source of commentary on
ethnic literature from the
perspective of Life as
literature & Literature as
life.

metaphors turned red
"Winning the West"
" Mexican as Passive"
" Indian is not rational
" Cowboys + Indians"